EDGE OF EXISTENCE

Edge of existence

species' last plea.

ALINE HAZLE

Spectra Enterprise

CONTENTS

TABLE OF CONTENT

Chapter 6: Biodiversity's Silent Quake

6.1 Delving into the broader impact of species loss on ecosystems.

6.2 Examining the cascading effects on other species, habitats, and even human communities.

6.3 Illustrating the concept of biodiversity as a stabilizing force.

Chapter 7: Endangered Symphony

7.1 Portraying the interconnectedness of species as a symphony.

7.2 Emphasizing the unique role each species plays in maintaining ecological harmony.

7.3 Discussing the consequences of losing certain "notes" in the symphony.

Chapter 8: Last Plea Dance

8.1 A closer look at species on the brink of extinction.

8.2 Stories of those hanging on by a thread and the critical interventions required.

8.3 Examining the ethical and moral dimensions of letting a species disappear.

Chapter 9: Conservation Harmony

9.1 Highlighting successful conservation stories and the restoration of balance.

9.2 Examining the potential for human intervention to heal and protect ecosystems.

9.3 Inspiring hope through concrete examples of recovery.

INTRODUCTION

In the tremendous embroidery of the universe, where the limits of reality obscure into the domain of the obscure, there exists a sensitive harmony wavering on the edge of presence. In the midst of the enormous expressive dance of stars and cosmic systems, on the immaterial light blue speck known as Earth, an orchestra of life unfurls with unrivaled variety. This complex dance of species, each with its one of a kind job and commitment, has woven a rich embroidery that traverses ages and landmasses.

In any case, as the hands of time steadily tick forward, the congruity of presence faces an exceptional conflict. The planet, our support and home to endless residing creatures, remains at the slope of an emergency - an emergency that rises above the ages of geographical ages and difficulties the actual substance of endurance for horde species. This is certainly not a simple section in that frame of mind of normal history; it is the pivotal turning point, the crescendo of a story that stretches from the early stage seepage to the time of man-made consciousness.

The Edge of Presence is definitely not an actual area yet a figurative wilderness where the battle for endurance escalates, where the beat of life beats in cadence with the existential danger that poses a potential threat. It is where species, extraordinary and little, end up in a frantic request for their proceeded with presence. This isn't a call for simple endurance; it is an orchestra of voices, a clamor of murmurs reverberating through the passageways of time, as species face a quickly impacting world.

In the huge breadth of Earth's set of experiences, ages have gone back and forth, seeing the ascent and fall of realms, the advancement of species, and the geographical change of scenes. However, the current age, set apart by the engraving of mankind, is one of unmatched outcome. The Anthropocene, as it is appropriately named, gives testimony regarding the extraordinary force of human movement - an impact that reaches out past simple impressions and reverberations through the sensitive environments that support life.

Humankind, blessed with knowledge and mechanical ability, has turned into a power fit for molding the predetermination of the whole biosphere. Notwithstanding, this newly discovered territory over nature has included some significant pitfalls - an expense that resounds across biological systems and causes qualms about the complex trap of life. The Edge of Presence is the stage whereupon this show unfurls, where the heroes are human as well as envelop a horde of animal categories, each assuming a crucial part in the many-sided embroidery of biodiversity.

As the wheels of progress turn and the walk of civilization pushes forward, the inadvertent blow-back caused upon the climate turns out to be progressively clear. Natural surroundings are demolished, environments disturbed, and species end up near the precarious edge of annihilation. The quick speed of industrialization, the constant quest for assets, and the unquenchable craving for development have driven various species to the edge, delivering them weak despite a changing environment and decreasing territories.

The ensemble of life, once agreeable, is currently interspersed by the forlorn cries of animals nearly disappearing until the end of time. The lessening quantities of notorious species, from superb elephants to confounding rhinoceroses, tell a story of human infringement and the dire requirement for protection. The Edge of Presence is definitely not a far off boondocks however a reality scratched in the battle for endurance of species that have graced the Earth for centuries.

However, the emergency reaches out past the alluring megafauna that catch our consideration and compassion. It saturates the secret domains of biodiversity, where endless life forms, frequently concealed and disregarded, assume fundamental parts in the multifaceted equilibrium of biological systems. From infinitesimal growths to subtle bugs, the biodiversity emergency projects a wide net, undermining the actual underpinnings of life as far as we might be concerned.

In this age of vulnerability, the idea of the Edge of Presence rises above the actual limits of the regular world. It reaches out into the shared mindset of humankind - a request for mindfulness, obligation, and activity. The destiny of species is complicatedly woven into the texture of human decisions, and the results of our activities echo through the multifaceted trap of life.

The keep going supplication of species on the Edge of Presence isn't a call for feel sorry for yet an invitation to battle. It coaxes mankind to rethink its relationship with the planet, to recognize the interconnectedness of all living things, and to perceive the common predetermination that ties us to the destiny of the normal world. It is a request for protection, maintainability, and an amicable concurrence that rises above the thin bounds of anthropocentrism.

As the account unfurls on the Edge of Presence, the sections are not foreordained; they are composed by our decisions today. Will we be the engineers of a future where biodiversity flourishes, biological systems thrive, and the orchestra of life reverberates with essentialness? Or on the other hand will we be the creators of a requiem, a mourn for animal groups lost and environments debased?

The Edge of Presence coaxes us to pick our way carefully, for the results of our choices reverberation through time, molding the heritage we leave for people in the future. Right now, the request of species turns into a mirror mirroring the quintessence of our mankind - our ability for compassion, our insight in stewardship, and our flexibility despite challenges.

The Edge of Presence is a cauldron where the speculative chemistry of sympathy, information, and activity can produce a future where the last supplication of species turns into an energizing sob for a world that values the variety of life. It is a call to embrace our job as caretakers of the planet, to proceed with caution on the Earth, and to guarantee that the orchestra of presence keeps on playing for a long time into the future.

CHAPTER 1

The Fragile Web

In the unpredictable dance of presence, the Delicate Web arises as a fragile embroidery that winds around together the strings of life, associating each living creature in an orchestra of relationship. This figurative web traverses environments, landmasses, and seas, making an intricate organization that supports the equilibrium of nature. A web has developed more than huge number of years, adjusting and interconnecting in manners that oppose human perception. However, this multifaceted web, which has endured the hardships of time, is presently confronting uncommon difficulties that compromise its actual pith.

At the core of the Delicate Web lies the idea of biodiversity - the amazing exhibit of life frames that occupy our planet. From the transcending redwoods to the minuscule creatures concealed in the dirt, every species assumes a one of a kind part in the fabulous embroidery of life. Biodiversity isn't simply a proportion of the sheer number of species however the mind boggling connections and communications that tight spot them together. It is the mysterious language of nature, a quiet exchange that supports biological systems and sustains the essentialness of the planet.

As the hands of time turn, the Delicate Web ends up extended and stressed by the tenacious tensions of human action. The fast speed of industrialization, unrestrained deforestation, contamination, and the warming environment have turned into the supposed quakes that take steps to disentangle the fragile strings of the web. Species, both known and unseen, are confronting the phantom of eradication at a disturbing rate, upsetting the multifaceted equilibrium that has advanced over centuries.

The Delicate Web is definitely not a uninvolved substance; a dynamic and versatile power answers the recurring pattern of normal cycles. In any case, the ongoing difficulties represent an existential danger that surpasses the web's ability for self-recharging. The deficiency of biodiversity, frequently alluded to as the 6th mass elimination, isn't simply an organic emergency yet a significant disturbance of the Delicate Web that supports life on The planet.

In the huge field of this perplexing web, each strand is a representation for the horde biological systems that make up the biosphere. From lavish rainforests to parched deserts, from the profundities of the seas to the transcending mountain tops, these environments are the establishment whereupon the Delicate Web is constructed. Every biological system harbors a novel assortment of animal groups adjusted to its particular circumstances, framing a mosaic of life that makes a versatile and interconnected entirety.

In any case, the Delicate Web is disentangling despite anthropogenic tensions. Deforestation, driven by the interest for wood, farming extension, and urbanization, is stripping the snare of its strands. The trimming tools reverberation through the rainforests, and as trees fall, the perplexing associations that once supported innumerable species are cut off. The repercussions reach out past the prompt loss of biodiversity; whole biological systems disintegrate, and the Delicate Web debilitates.

All the while, contamination arises as a quiet yet unavoidable danger. The release of contaminations high up, water, and soil disturbs the sensitive equilibrium of biological systems, harming the strands of the Delicate Web. From modern synthetics to plastic waste, human-created poisons pervade the climate, influencing species from the littlest microorganisms to the biggest hunters. The Delicate Web, once tough, presently bears the scars of pollution.

Environmental change, powered by the ignition of non-renewable energy sources and deforestation, creates a long shaded area over the Delicate Web. Climbing temperatures, outrageous climate occasions, and moving environment designs present difficulties that numerous species are unfit to confront. The interconnected idea of environments implies that an aggravation in one region can send shockwaves all through the whole web. The Delicate Web, woven through periods of solidness, is stressed by the unconventionality of an evolving environment.

In the profundities of seas, where an outsider universe of marvels unfurls, the Delicate Web faces special difficulties. Overfishing, living space annihilation, and the fermentation of seawater because of expanded carbon dioxide levels compromise marine environments. Coral reefs, dynamic center points of biodiversity, are fading and kicking the bucket as the sensitive harmony among corals and their advantageous green growth is upset. The Delicate Web, unpredictably associated with the seas, trembles under the heaviness of human effect.

As the Delicate Web unwinds, the outcomes reach out past the domains of nature. Human social orders, complicatedly connected to the strength of the biosphere, face the gamble of environmental breakdown. The arrangement of fundamental administrations, from clean water to fertilization of yields, depends on the working of environments. The Delicate Web, once underestimated, is uncovering its interconnected nature, and the delicacy of human prosperity becomes laced with the destiny of the normal world.

However, in the midst of the difficulties, there is trust. The Delicate Web, however stressed, still holds its flexibility. Preservation endeavors, feasible practices, and a developing consciousness of the interconnectedness of all life offer a flash of probability. Safeguarded regions, where biological systems can recover, become asylums for biodiversity. Rebuilding projects, planning to reweave the torn strands of the Delicate Web, grandstand the potential for human creativity and empathy.

The Delicate Web is certainly not a far off idea yet a reality that requests quick consideration. It requires a change in perspective in how mankind sees its relationship with the regular world. The affirmation that the destiny of species, environments, and the Delicate Web is interwoven with human decisions is the most vital move toward significant change. It is a call for stewardship, obligation, and a significant comprehension of the outcomes of our activities.

Training turns into a foundation in this groundbreaking excursion. The consciousness of biodiversity, environmental cycles, and the delicacy of the Delicate Web needs to worldwide pervade social orders. Informed residents, equipped with information, become advocates for change, affecting arrangements, and requesting maintainable practices. The Delicate Web, complicatedly attached to the selections of people, networks, and countries, turns into a material whereupon another story of concurrence is painted.

In the core of this story lies the acknowledgment that the Delicate Web isn't an item to be taken advantage of however a heritage to be protected. Native insight, customary biological information, and the voices of neighborhood networks, who have existed together with nature for ages, become priceless aides in this excursion. The Delicate Web, seen from the perspective of different viewpoints, turns into a common obligation that rises above boundaries and belief systems.

The Delicate Web, however confronting extraordinary difficulties, conveys inside it the potential for recovery. Rewilding endeavors, preservation drives, and supportable practices structure the fastens that repair the torn texture of the web. Cooperation turns into a key part, as countries, associations, and people join in an aggregate work to protect the Delicate Web for people in the future.

In the nightfall of this vital turning point, the Delicate Web allures mankind to adapt to the situation. It is a call to embrace a future where the sensitive strands of biodiversity are treasured, where environments flourish, and where the interconnectedness of all life isn't simply recognized however celebrated. The Delicate Web is a demonstration of the strength of nature, and in its protection lies the commitment of an agreeable concurrence among human-kind and the web that supports all of us.

1.1 Introduction to the interconnectedness of ecosystems and the delicate balance that sustains life.

In the terrific embroidery of nature, the interconnectedness of environments arises as a crucial rule that supports the sensitive equilibrium supporting life on The planet. Biological systems, those complicated snare of life where residing creatures collaborate with one another and their actual climate, structure the many-sided strings that wind around together the texture of our planet's biodiversity. This interconnectedness rises above geographic limits and stretches across mainlands, making an agreeable dance of life that has developed north of millions of years.

At the core of this many-sided dance lies the idea of environmental equilibrium — a fragile balance that guarantees the concurrence and common reliance of species inside a biological system. Every organic entity, from the littlest microorganisms to the dominant hunters, assumes an extraordinary part in keeping up with this equilibrium. It's a movement where each development, each communication, has an expanding influence, molding the elements of the whole framework.

Take, for example, a timberland biological system. Trees, with their transcending shades, give haven and natural surroundings to endless species — from birds and bugs to growths and vertebrates. The fallen leaves and rotting matter on the timberland floor add to supplement cycling, cultivating the development of plants and supporting the herbivores that brush upon them. Hunters, thusly, control the number of inhabitants in herbivores, forestalling overgrazing and keeping up with the soundness of the biological system. In this perplexing dance, the interconnectedness of species guarantees the woodland's versatility and imperativeness.

However, this sensitive equilibrium isn't restricted to earthly biological systems alone. Seas, with their tremendous breadths, harbor an interconnected world underneath the waves. Coral reefs, frequently alluded to as the "rainforests of the ocean," exemplify the reliance of species. Coral polyps, through a harmonious relationship with green growth, construct the mind boggling designs of reefs, giving sanctuary and favorable places to a horde of marine life. The interconnectedness of the reef biological system stretches out to untamed sea waters, where transitory species navigate great many miles, interfacing far off locales in a snare of life.

The idea of interconnectedness likewise stretches out to freshwater biological systems, where streams and lakes act as crucial conduits, connecting earthbound and oceanic conditions. Salmon, for instance, leave on incredible excursions from the sea to freshwater generating grounds, conveying supplements from the marine environment to sustain the encompassing area. This repetitive relocation isn't just a demonstration of the versatility of species yet an unmistakable representation of the mind boggling associations that support life across various biological systems.

As mankind progresses mechanically and extends its impression across the planet, the fragile equilibrium of interconnected biological systems faces phenomenal difficulties. Anthropogenic exercises, from deforestation and urbanization to contamination and environmental change, disturb the agreeable dance that has developed throughout land time. The results of such interruptions are broad, influencing the normal world as well as the prosperity of human social orders unpredictably connected to the administrations given by biological systems.

Deforestation, driven by the interest for lumber and the extension of farming area, destroys the complicated design of woods environments. The deficiency of trees decreases environment for endless species as well as disturbs the water cycle, prompting changes in precipitation designs and expanded weakness to catastrophic events. The interconnectedness of environments becomes clear as changes in a single region resonate across the worldwide environment framework.

Also, contamination, whether from modern releases, agrarian overflow, or plastic waste, rises above the limits of individual environments. Foreign substances brought into streams and seas gather in the tissues of organic entities, influencing species distant from the first source. The interconnectedness of biological systems, when a wellspring of strength, presently turns into a conductor for the spread of ecological corruption.

Environmental change, driven by the arrival of ozone harming substances from human exercises, intensifies the complexities of interconnected biological systems. Increasing temperatures, modified precipitation examples, and outrageous climate occasions overflow through biological systems, influencing the dissemination and conduct of species.

Coral reefs dye as sea temperatures climb, upsetting the sensitive equilibrium of these lively submerged biological systems. The interconnectedness of Earth's frameworks, from the air to the seas, highlights the criticalness of tending to the main drivers of environmental change.

Even with these difficulties, there is a developing acknowledgment of the need to reestablish and safeguard the interconnectedness of environments. Preservation endeavors, going from the foundation of safeguarded regions to local area drove drives, intend to protect the variety of life and keep up with the fragile equilibrium of biological systems. Rebuilding projects, whether zeroed in on reforestation, wetland recovery, or marine preservation, look to patch the strings of the mind boggling web that supports life.

Also, the attention to the significance of interconnected environments has penetrated worldwide talk. The idea is implanted in systems, for example, the Show on Organic Variety, which perceives the need to save environments and advance manageable utilization of their parts. The interconnectedness of biodiversity, environment, and human prosperity is at the very front of conversations on worldwide supportability, underscoring the fundamental job biological systems play in forming the eventual fate of our planet.

Teaching social orders about the complexities of interconnected environments turns into a foundation in encouraging an aggregate comprehension of our job as stewards of the Earth. Information engages people and networks to pursue informed decisions that add to the protection and rebuilding of biological systems. It advances an ethos of capable conjunction, where the sensitive equilibrium of nature is adored, and the interconnectedness of all life is recognized.

In the tremendous ensemble of life, the interconnectedness of biological systems is both a significant truth and a source of inspiration. It welcomes us to perceive our place inside the complex dance of nature, where our choices reverberate across the strings of the web that supports us. As overseers of this planet, we are shared with the obligation with safeguard the fragile equilibrium of interconnected biological systems, guaranteeing that the embroidery of life stays lively for a long time into the future. In embracing this obligation, we weave a story of conjunction, concordance, and worship for the interconnected web that joins generally living creatures.

1.2 Overview of the current state of biodiversity and the alarming rate of species decline.

Against the setting of Earth's unpredictable environments, the present status of biodiversity portrays an unfurling emergency.

Biodiversity, the entirety of every living creature and the environments they occupy, is confronting remarkable difficulties that undermine the actual texture of life on our planet. The disturbing pace of species decline, set apart by eradications and populace decreases, creates a shaded area over the multifaceted embroidery that has developed more than large number of years.

The expression "biodiversity" envelops the wealth and assortment of life in the entirety of its structures, from the smallest organisms to the most magnificent animals, and from the profundities of the seas to the transcending pinnacles of mountains. Biodiversity isn't simply a proportion of the sheer number of species; it incorporates the unpredictable collaborations and interdependencies that weave environments together. The fragile equilibrium permits life to prosper, offering fundamental types of assistance like fertilization, water refinement, and environment guideline.

Be that as it may, this complicated equilibrium is under attack. The present status of biodiversity mirrors an emergency that has been exacerbated by human exercises. The pace of species decline is disturbing, and the results of losing biodiversity stretch out a long ways past the vanishing of individual species. The wellbeing of environments, the strength of normal cycles, and the solidness of the planet's environment are unpredictably connected to the condition of biodiversity.

One of the essential drivers of the disturbing pace of species decline is natural surroundings misfortune. Human exercises, from horticulture and urbanization to logging and framework advancement, have changed scenes at an uncommon scale. As territories disappear, species lose their homes, disturbing the multifaceted connections that have developed over centuries. The discontinuity of natural surroundings separates populaces, conveying species more defenseless against intimidations, for example, infection and environmental change.

Deforestation, specifically, stands apart as a significant supporter of environment misfortune. The change of woods into horticultural land, logging tasks, and framework projects have prompted the obliteration of basic territories for endless species. Notorious environments, like the Amazon rainforest, are seeing quick deforestation, bringing about the deficiency of biodiversity on an incredible scale. The multifaceted trap of life that once flourished in these backwoods is disentangling, and the outcomes are resonating all around the world.

Notwithstanding environment misfortune, the disturbing pace of species decline is driven by different elements, including contamination, overexploitation, and environmental change. Contamination, whether from modern releases, agrarian spillover, or plastic waste, invades biological systems, sullying air, water, and soil. This contamination upsets the fragile equilibrium of biological systems, influencing species across the pecking order and undermining their capacity to flourish.

Overexploitation of regular assets, driven by unreasonable practices, represents an immediate danger to various species. From overfishing in the seas to poaching of notable natural life for the unlawful untamed life exchange, the tireless quest for assets is driving numerous species to the edge of elimination. The unpredictable connections that once controlled populaces and kept up with biological equilibrium are disturbed, prompting flowing impacts on whole environments.

Environmental change, energized by human exercises like the consuming of non-renewable energy sources and deforestation, fuels the disturbing pace of species decline. Climbing temperatures, changes in precipitation examples, and more successive outrageous climate occasions present difficulties that numerous species are unfit to confront. The interconnected idea of environments implies that an aggravation in one region can have flowing impacts on the whole snare of life.

The outcomes of the disturbing pace of species decline reach out to mankind. Biodiversity misfortune is definitely not a far off issue bound to far off environments; it in a roundabout way affects human prosperity. The arrangement of fundamental administrations, like clean water, fruitful soil, and fertilization of harvests, depends on the wellbeing of environments. The deficiency of biodiversity subverts these administrations, presenting dangers to food security, water quality, and in general natural dependability.

Moreover, the social and tasteful worth of biodiversity couldn't possibly be more significant. Numerous people group all over the planet have profound social connections to the regular world, depending on conventional information and practices went down through ages. The deficiency of interesting species and biological systems disintegrates social variety and decreases the profound and stylish associations that people have with the regular world.

In light of the disturbing pace of species decline, the worldwide local area has perceived the requirement for pressing activity. Global structures and arrangements, for example, the Show on Organic Variety, intend to address the hidden drivers of biodiversity misfortune and advance protection and supportable utilization of natural variety. Nonetheless, the hole between strategy expectations and on-the-ground execution stays a huge test.

Preservation endeavors, going from the foundation of safeguarded regions to local area drove drives, assume a critical part in tending to the disturbing pace of species decline. These endeavors expect to shield basic living spaces, safeguard imperiled species, and advance reasonable practices that fit with the necessities of environments. Preservation likewise includes bringing issues to light and encouraging a feeling of obligation among people and networks.

Logical exploration and checking programs are fundamental parts of figuring out the present status of biodiversity and creating compelling protection methodologies. Through progressions in innovation and information assortment, researchers can follow changes in populaces, survey the strength of biological systems, and recognize regions not looking so great. This information is critical for informed direction and versatile administration.

1.3 Setting the stage for the urgency of conservation efforts.

In the immense venue of Earth's environments, the desperation of preservation endeavors becomes the dominant focal point as the spotlight radiates on the heightening dangers confronting biodiversity. The mind boggling dance of life, spreading over mainlands and seas, is confronting extraordinary disturbances that request prompt consideration and deliberate activity. As the drape ascends on this crucial second, it turns out to be progressively evident that the destiny of biological systems, species, and the sensitive equilibrium of nature depends on the earnestness with which humankind tends to the difficulties that pose a potential threat on the protection stage.

At the core of the earnestness lies the acknowledgment that we are at an intersection, where the decisions today will resonate through the passageways of time. Biodiversity, the lively mosaic of life that embellishes our planet, is disentangling at a disturbing speed. The setting to this unfurling show is set apart by territory annihilation, contamination, overexploitation, and the approaching ghost of environmental change. Every one of these dangers, powered by human exercises, is a vital participant in the story of biodiversity misfortune, and their consolidated effect is driving environments to the edge.

Territory obliteration, a constant power driven by farming, urbanization, and foundation improvement, is an essential bad guy in the criticalness of preservation endeavors. The transformation of regular scenes into human-ruled conditions disturbs the sensitive equilibrium that has developed over centuries. Species lose their homes, and the perplexing trap of connections that supports biological systems is cut off. As backwoods fall, wetlands disappear, and coral reefs dye, the direness of safeguarding what remains becomes central.

Even with natural surroundings annihilation, whole environments are very nearly breakdown. The Amazon rainforest, frequently alluded to as the "lungs of the Earth," faces extraordinary deforestation, compromising its ability to manage worldwide environment designs. Coral reefs, essential center points of biodiversity, are capitulating to climbing ocean temperatures and fermentation. The desperation is highlighted by the acknowledgment that these environments, when remembered to be strong, are wavering on the edge of hopeless harm.

Contamination, one more considerable enemy in the preservation show, further enhances the criticalness of defensive measures. Impurities, going from modern synthetic substances to plastic waste, penetrate the air, water, and soil, resulting in a path of obliteration afterward. The results are sweeping, influencing species at each trophic level and pervading environments. From harmed waterways to trash flung seas, the earnestness of tending to contamination is clear in the apparent scars left on the normal world.

Overexploitation of normal assets arises as a third bad guy in the earnestness of protection endeavors. Impractical practices, driven by the interest for wood, fish, and natural life items, are driving various species to the edge of annihilation. Notable creatures, from elephants to tigers, face the danger of poaching for their ivory, skins, and body parts. Overfishing drains marine populaces, disturbing the sensitive equilibrium of sea environments. The earnestness is obvious as the determined quest for assets undermines individual species as well as the strength of whole environments.

Environmental change, an approaching presence on the preservation stage, adds a layer of intricacy to the direness of defensive activities. The consuming of petroleum derivatives and deforestation discharge ozone harming substances, prompting climbing temperatures, changed precipitation examples, and more incessant outrageous climate occasions. The ramifications for biodiversity are significant, with species confronting the test of adjusting to quickly changing circumstances or moving to additional appropriate territories. The direness lies in the acknowledgment that environmental change worsens existing dangers, putting forth protection attempts significantly more goal.

As the earnestness of protection endeavors turns out to be progressively clear, the results of inaction pose a potential threat. The deficiency of biodiversity has flowing impacts that stretch out past the regular world, affecting human social orders in manners that are both immediate and circuitous. The arrangement of fundamental administrations, from clean water to fertilization of yields, depends on the strength of biological systems. The desperation is evident as the debasement of biological systems presents dangers to food security, water quality, and generally speaking ecological dependability.

Additionally, the earnestness of preservation endeavors is interwoven with the social and otherworldly associations that networks all over the planet have with the normal world. Native people groups, specifically, frequently depend on the biodiversity of their environmental elements for food, medication, and social practices. The direness lies in perceiving and regarding the assorted manners by which various networks cooperate with and rely upon biological systems. The deficiency of biodiversity dissolves social variety and reduces the otherworldly and tasteful associations that people have with the regular world.

Because of the criticalness of preservation endeavors, a developing melody of voices is calling for groundbreaking activity. Peaceful accords, for example, the Show on Organic Variety, set up for composed endeavors to address the fundamental drivers of biodiversity misfortune. The direness is reflected in the worldwide affirmation that the ideal opportunity for way of talking alone has passed; considerable and quick activity is expected to alleviate the dangers confronting environments.

Preservation endeavors, going from the foundation of safeguarded regions to local area drove drives, are basic entertainers in the earnestness of protecting biodiversity. These endeavors intend to shield basic environments, safeguard imperiled species, and advance manageable practices that fit with the requirements of biological systems. The criticalness of preservation becomes clear as these drives endeavor to turn around the tide of territory annihilation, contamination, overexploitation, and environmental change.

Logical exploration and observing projects assume an essential part in understanding the desperation of preservation needs. Through headways in innovation and information assortment, researchers can follow changes in populaces, survey the soundness of environments, and distinguish regions in rough shape. The criticalness lies in the information that educated direction and versatile administration are fundamental apparatuses in the protection tool compartment.

Training arises as a key part in the direness of protection endeavors. Bringing issues to light about the worth of biodiversity, the dangers it faces, and the significance of preservation cultivates a feeling of obligation among people and networks. The earnestness is highlighted by the acknowledgment that an educated populace is bound to go with decisions that add to the conservation of environments.

CHAPTER 2

Icons at Risk

In the advancing account of Earth's biodiversity, certain species stand apart as symbols — sublime animals that represent the extravagance and variety of life on our planet. In any case, against the scenery of raising dangers, for example, environment obliteration, environmental change, and poaching, these symbols are presently considered "Symbols In danger." The predicament of these magnetic species fills in as a powerful sign of the critical requirement for protection endeavors to shield individual species as well as the whole embroidery of life.

One such symbol in danger is the grand African Elephant (Loxodonta africana). Overshadowing the African savannah, these delicate goliaths have meandered the landmass for centuries, molding environments through their complicated social designs and scene adjusting ways of behaving. However, the ivory exchange stays an impressive danger, driving poaching that pulverizes elephant populaces. The Symbols In danger stage uncovers a heartbreaking oddity where the sheer greatness of these animals makes them powerless to human voracity. Preservation endeavors pointed toward checking poaching, destroying unlawful untamed life exchange organizations, and laying out safeguarded regions are fundamental in getting the fate of African Elephants.

In the maritime domain, the endangered status of the Incomparable Obstruction Reef's dynamic coral environments puts the famous coral developments themselves in danger. The unpredictable dance of varieties underneath the waves, made by corals and their cooperative green growth, is under danger because of climbing ocean temperatures, coral fading, and sea fermentation — all outcomes of environmental change. The Symbols In danger spotlight accentuates the pressing requirement for worldwide activity to moderate environmental change, lessen fossil fuel byproducts, and safeguard marine conditions. Protection drives that emphasis on coral rebuilding and maintainable practices add to the continuous battle to safeguard these notorious submerged scenes.

The grand Bengal Tiger (Panthera tigris) is another notorious species confronting inescapable gamble. Once wandering across tremendous regions of the Indian subcontinent, the Bengal Tiger's populaces have dwindled because of living space misfortune and uncontrolled poaching. The desperation in protecting this famous huge feline untruths not just in saving an image of solidarity and effortlessness yet additionally in keeping up with the fragile equilibrium of environments. Preservation endeavors include making safeguarded natural surroundings, executing against poaching measures, and advancing concurrence among people and tigers. The Symbols In danger account prompts reflection on the more extensive ramifications of losing such cornerstone species from their normal living spaces.

Polar bears (Ursus maritimus), the alluring symbols of the Cold, are at the very front of environmental change influences. As ocean ice decreases because of an unnatural weather change, polar bears face difficulties in chasing after seals, their essential prey. The Symbols In danger account highlights the weakness of these eminent animals even with natural changes. Preservation endeavors incorporate measures to battle environmental change, safeguard fundamental living spaces, and moderate human-bear clashes. The situation of polar bears fills in as an obvious update that the effects of environmental change resound across species, biological systems, and, at last, the whole planet.

The mysterious mountain gorillas (Gorilla beringei) of Focal Africa's lavish rainforests exemplify the weakness of extraordinary primates in the Symbols In danger situation. These delicate goliaths, imparting a surprising hereditary family relationship to people, are compromised by territory misfortune, poaching, and sicknesses communicated by people. Preservation drives zeroing in on living space security, hostile to poaching measures, and capable ecotourism offer a good omen for the endurance of mountain gorillas. Their unstable presence features the complex equilibrium expected to save biodiversity, especially for species near the precarious edge of annihilation.

The vaquita (Phocoena sinus), the littlest and generally imperiled cetacean, embodies the Symbols In danger story in the domain of marine life. With an expected populace in the simple twofold digits, the vaquita faces termination fundamentally because of bycatch in unlawful gillnets used to get one more imperiled animal categories, the totoaba fish. The earnestness in safeguarding the vaquita reaches out past a solitary animal varieties — it mirrors the more extensive requirement for manageable fishing rehearses, marine protection, and global participation. The Symbols In danger focus on the vaquita highlights the interconnectedness of marine environments and the sensitive equilibrium expected to safeguard marine biodiversity.

The notable orangutan (Pongo spp.) species, local to the rainforests of Borneo and Sumatra, is facing the double danger of environment annihilation and unlawful exchange. As palm oil estates extend, the orangutans' timberland homes are quickly vanishing, driving them nearer to the edge of elimination. The Symbols In danger story for orangutans features the basic requirement for preservation endeavors that address both living space security and the palm oil industry's maintainability. The predicament of orangutans fills in as a microcosm of the more extensive test in blending human improvement with biodiversity protection.

An impactful illustration of a notorious bird in danger is the California Condor (Gymnogyps californianus). With a wingspan surpassing nine feet, these wonderful birds were near the precarious edge of eradication in the late twentieth 100 years because of lead harming and territory misfortune. Concentrated protection endeavors, including hostage rearing projects and lead ammo boycotts, have taken huge steps in saving the California Condor. The Symbols In danger story for these goliath birds highlights the significance of proactive preservation measures and the potential for fruitful recuperation programs when purposeful endeavors are embraced.

In the core of Africa's lavish rainforests, the Cross Stream Gorilla (gorilla diehli) becomes the dominant focal point as a notorious species confronting approaching gamble. With a populace assessed at only a couple hundred people, this subspecies of gorilla defies dangers, for example, living space misfortune and fracture because of farming and human settlement. The Symbols In danger story for the Cross Waterway Gorilla underlines the requirement for reasonable land-use rehearses, local area commitment, and worldwide joint effort to get the fate of these fundamentally imperiled primates.

The slippery snow panther (Panthera uncia), possessing the high-elevation scenes of Focal and South Asia, embodies the Symbols In danger situation in the domain of large felines. Poaching, retaliatory killings by herders, and living space fracture present serious dangers to the endurance of these wonderful hunters.

Preservation endeavors center around relieving human-untamed life clashes, reinforcing against poaching measures, and laying out safeguarded regions. The direness in safeguarding snow panthers stretches out past saving a charming animal types — it envelops the protection of novel mountain biological systems and the fragile equilibrium they exemplify.

The jeopardized leatherback ocean turtle (Dermochelys coriacea), the biggest of all ocean turtle species, addresses the Symbols In danger situation on the planet's seas. These old sailors face dangers from environmental change, natural surroundings misfortune, and fisheries bycatch. Preservation drives center around safeguarding settling locales, executing turtle-accommodating fishing rehearses, and tending to the effects of environmental change on marine biological systems. The direness in protecting leatherback ocean turtles repeats the more extensive requirement for marine preservation and feasible fisheries practices to save the biodiversity of our seas.

2.1 Highlighting charismatic and emblematic species facing the edge of existence.

In the immense material of Earth's biodiversity, certain species arise as appealling and symbolic envoys of the regular world, dazzling hearts and brains with their one of a kind stunner and importance. Nonetheless, the charm of these animals is joined by a sobering reality — they are confronting the edge of presence, standing up to dangers that push them towards the verge of eradication. The situation of these charming and meaningful species fills in as a strong sign of the desperation and obligation mankind bears in saving the miracles of our planet.

At the front of this story stands the charming Sumatran orangutan (Pongo abelii). These shaggy-haired primates, local to the lavish rainforests of Sumatra, Indonesia, typify the delicate goliaths of the gorilla family. However, their appealling presence gives a false representation of the unforgiving truth of territory obliteration and unlawful pet exchange. As palm oil manors grow and timberlands contract, Sumatran orangutans face a lessening scene, driving them unsafely near the brink of presence. Preservation endeavors, including environment insurance and recovery focuses, are vital to get a future for these notable primates and the biodiversity-rich biological systems they possess.

In the core of Africa, the symbolic mountain gorilla (Gorilla beringei) orders consideration. Settled in the fog covered slants of the Virunga Mountains, these wonderful animals are both an image of the wild and a demonstration of the fragile equilibrium expected for their endurance.

Their appealling nature, portrayed by familial bonds and many-sided social designs, stands out pointedly from the dangers they face — living space misfortune, poaching, and illness transmission from people. The edge of presence for mountain gorillas highlights the significance of all encompassing preservation methodologies that address both untamed life assurance and the prosperity of encompassing networks.

The magnetic Bengal tiger (Panthera tigris) remains as a notorious image of solidarity and grandness. Once uninhibitedly meandering across the huge scenes of the Indian subcontinent, these enormous felines are currently restricted to divided living spaces, their numbers decreasing because of environment misfortune and poaching. The edge of presence for Bengal tigers is an unmistakable sign of the unpredictable equilibrium expected to safeguard cornerstone species and keep up with environment wellbeing. Preservation drives, for example, laying out safeguarded regions and against poaching measures, are basic to guaranteeing the endurance of these alluring cats.

In the frosty domains of the Icy, the polar bear (Ursus maritimus) rules as the significant symbol of the frozen wild. These considerable hunters explore the ocean ice looking for seals, epitomizing the strength and versatility expected to get by in cruel conditions. Be that as it may, the edge of presence for polar bears is honed by the fast loss of ocean ice because of environmental change. As their frosty stages shrivel, polar bears face difficulties in chasing after food, endangering their endurance. Preservation endeavors should zero in on alleviating environmental change influences, safeguarding basic living spaces, and encouraging conjunction among people and polar bears.

The alluring and slippery snow panther (Panthera uncia) occupies the high-elevation scenes of Focal and South Asia, representing the persona of rocky districts. With its thick fur and spotted coat, the snow panther explores rough landscapes with unmatched effortlessness. However, the edge of presence for these notorious enormous felines is set apart by poaching, retaliatory killings by herders, and territory discontinuity. Preservation drives, enveloping local area commitment, hostile to poaching measures, and laying out safeguarded regions, are basic to get a future for snow panthers and the novel environments they occupy.

Underneath the waves, the significant leatherback ocean turtle (Dermochelys coriacea) coasts through the sea, addressing the antiquated sailors of the ocean. As the biggest of all ocean turtle species, leatherbacks have crossed seas for a long period of time. Be that as it may, the edge of presence for these charming animals is highlighted by dangers, for example, environmental change, territory misfortune, and fisheries bycatch. Preservation endeavors should zero in on safeguarding settling destinations, carrying out turtle-accommodating fishing rehearses, and tending to the more extensive difficulties looked by marine biological systems.

The charming African elephant (Loxodonta africana), with its magnificent tusks and familial securities, typifies the loftiness of untamed life on the African savannah. However, the edge of presence for African elephants is portrayed by the deceptive poaching emergency driven by the interest for ivory. As poachers focus on these delicate goliaths, in addition to the fact that singular elephants lost are, however the many-sided social designs of elephant crowds are upset. Protection endeavors, including hostile to poaching measures and local area commitment, are vital in getting the fate of these symbolic pachyderms.

In the domain of avian marvels, the charming California condor (Gymnogyps californianus) takes off above rough scenes, representing the endeavors of preservationists to save an animal varieties near the very edge of termination. The edge of presence for these epic birds was once set apart by lead harming and living space misfortune. In any case, escalated protection programs, including hostage rearing and lead ammo boycotts, have prompted critical steps in the recuperation of California condors. Their story fills in as a motivation, delineating the potential for fruitful preservation endeavors when decided move is made.

In the sea-going domains, the vaquita (Phocoena sinus) remains as a minuscule porpoise on the edge of presence. With an expected populace in the simple twofold digits, the vaquita faces termination principally because of bycatch in unlawful gillnets used to get one more imperiled animal groups, the totoaba fish. The appealling vaquita addresses the interconnectedness of marine environments and the desperation in tending to unreasonable fishing rehearses. Protection drives zeroing in on the vaquita highlight the requirement for worldwide cooperation and feasible marine administration.

The alluring ruler butterfly (Danaus plexippus) attempts an exceptional relocation, dazzling spectators with its dynamic tones and fragile wings. However, the edge of presence for these notable pollinators is set apart by territory misfortune, pesticide use, and environmental change influences. Preservation endeavors, including the assurance of rearing and overwintering environments, are significant in guaranteeing the endurance of ruler butterflies and the imperative job they play in fertilization.

The meaningful Cross Waterway gorilla (gorilla diehli) of Focal Africa becomes the overwhelming focus as a notable species confronting inevitable gamble. With a populace assessed at only a couple hundred people, this sub-species of gorilla defies dangers, for example, environment misfortune and fracture because of farming and human settlement. The edge of presence for the Cross Stream gorilla underlines the requirement for supportable land-use rehearses, local area commitment, and worldwide cooperation to get the fate of these fundamentally imperiled primates.

In the general story of charming and symbolic species confronting the edge of presence, the earnestness of preservation endeavors turns into a focal topic. These species, images of Earth's rich biodiversity, act as couriers, pointing out the more extensive difficulties of territory annihilation, poaching, environmental change, and unreasonable practices. The obligation lies with mankind to go about as stewards of the planet, carrying out compelling preservation measures, encouraging concurrence with natural life, and tending to the main drivers of biodiversity misfortune. As we explore the fragile harmony among progress and protection, the tales of these charming and significant species act as signals, directing us towards a future where the miracles of the regular world persevere for a long time into the future.

2.2 Iconic animals and their role in ecosystems.

In the perplexing embroidery of Earth's biological systems, certain creatures arise as symbols — representative figures that assume significant parts in forming the equilibrium and elements of their separate surroundings. These notable creatures, frequently considered cornerstone species, hold an extraordinary importance as their presence or nonappearance can significantly affect the whole environment. From huge hunters to humble pollinators, these animals add to the complex dance of life, featuring the interconnectedness and flexibility of the normal world.

The notorious African Elephant (Loxodonta africana), with its glorious presence and familial bonds, fills in as a cornerstone animal varieties in different African biological systems. These delicate monsters, frequently alluded to as "environment engineers," assume a pivotal part in forming scenes. Through their taking care of propensities and development designs, elephants impact vegetation structure and make living spaces for different species. They are central members in keeping up with biodiversity, advancing plant variety, and making water sources by searching for water in dry riverbeds. The shortfall of elephants can prompt flowing impacts, influencing plant and creature networks and adjusting the actual texture of the biological systems they possess.

Likewise, the charming Bengal Tiger (Panthera tigris) expects the job of a cornerstone animal types in the Indian subcontinent. As dominant hunters, Bengal tigers control prey populaces, forestalling overgrazing and keeping up with the equilibrium of the biological system. Their presence impacts the way of behaving of herbivores, molding vegetation designs and advancing biodiversity. Tigers additionally add to the soundness of woods by controlling the number of inhabitants in herbivores, forestalling territory corruption. Preservation endeavors pointed toward safeguarding Bengal tigers have more extensive ramifications, for the actual species as well as for the whole environment they possess.

In the core of Africa's lavish rainforests, the meaningful mountain gorilla (Gorilla beringei) assumes a basic part as a cornerstone animal types. These delicate goliaths are fundamental for seed dispersal, as they consume leafy foods across the woods, saving seeds in various areas. The presence of mountain gorillas adds to the recovery and variety of plant species, impacting the general design of the woods. In addition, their social ways of behaving, like prepping and correspondence, have flowing impacts on the prosperity of the whole gorilla bunch, encouraging strength inside the environment.

The magnetic polar bear (Ursus maritimus), a symbol of the Cold, holds a novel natural job in its bone chilling living space. As dominant hunters of the ocean ice, polar bears basically go after seals. Their reliance on ocean ice for hunting makes them vital to the marine environment. Polar bears are signs of the wellbeing of Cold environments, reflecting changes in ocean ice conditions and the accessibility of prey species. The protection of polar bears has more extensive ramifications for the whole Cold food web, impacting the appropriation and wealth of different marine species.

In the hilly scenes of Focal and South Asia, the subtle snow panther (Panthera uncia) expects the job of a cornerstone animal types. As top hunters, snow panthers assist with managing the number of inhabitants in prey species, forestalling overgrazing and keeping up with the equilibrium of delicate mountain environments. Their presence likewise in a roundabout way helps more modest carnivores by restricting contest with different hunters. Preservation endeavors zeroed in on safeguarding snow panthers add to the general well-being and flexibility of high-height biological systems.

Underneath the waves, the symbolic leatherback ocean turtle (Dermochelys coriacea) assumes a significant part in marine environments. As transitory species, leatherback turtles add to the appropriation of supplements across various maritime areas. Their taking care of propensities assist with controlling jellyfish populaces, forestalling episodes that could upset the equilibrium of marine biological systems. Leatherbacks additionally impact ocean side vegetation through their settling exercises, making environments for other waterfront species. The preservation of leatherback ocean turtles is fundamental for saving the biodiversity and usefulness of marine conditions.

In the earthly domain, the magnetic California condor (Gymnogyps californianus) expects an exceptional natural job. As foragers, condors assume an imperative part in environment wellbeing by tidying up flesh and forestalling the spread of sicknesses. Their capacity to cover immense distances looking for food adds to the dispersal of supplements and impacts the arrangement of plant and creature networks. The protection of California condors shields the actual species as well as has flowing impacts on the elements of the environments they occupy.

The famous ruler butterfly (Danaus plexippus) fills in as a wonderful pollinator, assuming a pivotal part in supporting plant variety and environment efficiency. As these butterflies relocate across North America, they fertilize various blooming plants, guaranteeing the generation of various species. Ruler butterflies are particularly known for their job in pollinating milkweed plants, whereupon their hatchlings depend. The protection of ruler butterflies is interwoven with the conservation of fertilization administrations and the soundness of assorted plant networks.

In the tremendous maritime territories, the magnetic vaquita (Phocoena sinus) assumes a part as a sentinel animal groups in the Bay of California. As the littlest and most jeopardized cetacean, the vaquita's decay signals more extensive issues inside marine biological systems. The vaquita's territory covers with that of the totoaba fish, prompting its accidental ensnarement in unlawful gillnets. Preservation endeavors to safeguard the vaquita reach out past the actual species, tending to unreasonable fishing rehearses and the more extensive wellbeing of marine conditions.

The meaningful Cross Stream gorilla (gorilla diehli) of Focal Africa expects a basic environmental job inside its woodland living space. As seed dispersers, these gorillas add to the recovery and variety of plant species. Their scrounging and development designs impact the construction of the woods, making microhabitats that benefit different species. The protection of Cross Stream gorillas has suggestions for the wellbeing and flexibility of the rainforest biological systems they occupy.

2.3 Exploring the emotional and ecological impact of losing these species.

The deficiency of famous species, those magnetic and significant animals that have come to represent the extravagance and variety of Earth's environments, resonates a long ways past the domain of biological ramifications. It rises above logical investigation and dives into the profound and social aspects, making a permanent imprint on mankind's association with the normal world. As these species waver on the edge of presence, the close to home and natural effect of their potential vanishing illustrates the interconnectedness between the destiny of notable species and the prosperity of the planet.

Inwardly, the likely termination of notable species brings out a significant feeling of distress, distress, and misfortune. These animals, frequently woven into the texture of social stories and mankind's set of experiences, hold an exceptional spot in our shared perspective.

The African Elephant, with its superb presence and familial bonds, is worshipped for its environmental job as well as an image of shrewdness, strength, and familial ties in different societies. The possibility of losing such a glorious and socially huge species delivers a profound feeling of trouble, grieving the expected destruction of a living image that has propelled wonderment and deference for ages.

Additionally, the likely vanishing of the Bengal Tiger, epitomizing strength and grandness, conveys close to home weight that reaches out past its biological importance. Tigers have been venerated in folklore, old stories, and workmanship across different societies, representing power, mental fortitude, and excellence. The close to home effect of losing such a notorious species rises above borders and social limits, resounding with individuals overall who track down motivation and association in the appealling presence of these enormous felines.

The mountain gorilla, settled in the fog covered slants of Focal Africa, holds an extraordinary spot in the hearts of many. The close to home association with these delicate monsters isn't exclusively founded on their natural significance as seed dispersers and powerhouses of woodland structure yet additionally on their exceptional likenesses to people. Their familial bonds, expressive countenances, and social collaborations inspire sympathy and a significant comprehension of the interconnectedness among people and the regular world. The likely loss of mountain gorillas hits home that resounds on both a profound and compassionate level.

The situation of the polar bear in the quickly changing Icy scene represents the human-actuated influences on the climate. As these notorious animals explore contracting ocean ice as they continued looking for food, their battle turns into a strong representation for the more extensive difficulties of environmental change. The close to home reaction to the possible loss of polar bears mirrors a profound worry for the outcomes of human activities on the very species that have adjusted to life in the cruelest conditions on The planet.

The snow panther, tricky and secretive, typifies the soul of high-height mountain biological systems. Its potential vanishing not just connotes the departure of a charming enormous feline yet in addition undermines the fragile equilibrium of biological systems it possesses. The close to home effect of losing such an image of versatility and flexibility reflects the more extensive worries about the delicacy of rocky locales despite environmental change and human exercises.

Underneath the waves, the possible termination of the leatherback ocean turtle raises profound worries about the weakness of old sailors in the seas. These old animals, with their great size and transitory examples, associate far off maritime domains.

The profound effect originates from the acknowledgment that the misfortune of leatherback ocean turtles addresses not just the downfall of an animal varieties with inborn worth yet additionally the debasement of marine biological systems on a worldwide scale. The close to home reaction to the expected vanishing of these famous turtles mirrors a well established worry for the wellbeing and flexibility of the world's seas.

The charming California condor, when near the precarious edge of elimination, conveys with it a story of preservation achievement. The profound effect of losing these enormous birds, with their great wingspans and rummaging ways of behaving, wouldn't just mean a difficulty in protection endeavors yet additionally hose the expectation that species can recuperate from the edge. The close to home reverberation of the California condor's potential vanishing highlights the delicate idea of species recuperation and the continuous difficulties looked by imperiled natural life.

The significant ruler butterfly, with its energetic varieties and phenomenal relocation, catches the creative mind of individuals all over the planet. The likely loss of this famous pollinator raises close to home worries about the delicacy of biological systems and the unpredictable snare of connections that depend on fertilization administrations. The profound effect is entwined with the acknowledgment that the vanishing of ruler butterflies wouldn't just mean the departure of an outwardly staggering animal groups yet additionally upset the environments they add to through their fundamental job in plant proliferation.

In the huge maritime spans, the expected elimination of the vaquita, the littlest and generally jeopardized cetacean, conveys profound weight that reaches out past its minute size. The predicament of the vaquita reflects more extensive worries about unreasonable fishing rehearses and the effects of human exercises on marine life. The close to home effect of losing such a little porpoise repeats the desperation of resolving fundamental issues in marine protection and the requirement for worldwide collaboration to shield the wellbeing of sea environments.

The imperiled Cross Stream gorilla, with its restricted populace in the rainforests of Focal Africa, holds both environmental and close to home importance. The possible loss of this subspecies stresses the weakness of one of a kind environments and the significance of saving biodiversity notwithstanding living space obliteration and human infringement. The profound effect of losing the Cross Stream gorilla highlights the requirement for manageable land-use practices and global coordinated effort to safeguard the final populaces of these fundamentally jeopardized primates.

On a more extensive scale, the close to home effect of losing famous species isn't bound to individual species yet stretches out to the more extensive loss of biodiversity. Every species assumes an extraordinary part in the unpredictable trap of life, adding to the versatility and usefulness of biological systems. The profound reaction to the expected eradication of notable species mirrors a firmly established worry for the disentangling of this multifaceted web and the outcomes it holds for the eventual fate of life on The planet.

Naturally, the deficiency of notable species conveys significant ramifications for the equilibrium and usefulness of environments. Cornerstone species, like the African Elephant and Bengal Tiger, apply lopsided impacts on their environments, directing prey populaces and forming vegetation elements. The expected vanishing of these cornerstone species can set off flowing impacts, prompting uneven characters in food networks, changed vegetation designs, and disturbances in environmental cycles.

For example, the deficiency of African Elephants could bring about uncontrolled vegetation development and changed plant species organization, influencing the variety of herbivores and different species reliant upon the accessibility of assorted vegetation. Also, the possible eradication of Bengal Tigers could prompt an excess of herbivores, setting off natural surroundings corruption and adversely influencing plant networks. The far reaching influences of losing cornerstone species stretch out to different species inside their biological systems, making a cascading type of influence that can eventually undermine whole natural networks.

In marine environments, the likely eradication of the leatherback ocean turtle could disturb the equilibrium of jellyfish populaces, as leatherbacks assume an essential part in controlling jellyfish overflow. The shortfall of these turtles might prompt an expansion in jellyfish, adversely affecting fish populaces and influencing the general soundness of marine biological systems. The natural outcomes of losing cornerstone species like the leatherback ocean turtle stretch out past their singular effect on shape the elements of whole maritime food networks.

The profound and biological effect of losing famous species is entwined with more extensive issues of environment misfortune, environmental change, poaching, and unreasonable human exercises. The expected termination of these magnetic and meaningful animals fills in as an unmistakable advance notice, encouraging mankind to rethink its relationship with the regular world and focus on preservation endeavors. The profound reverberation of these misfortunes features the inherent worth of biodiversity and the dire need to address the main drivers of species decline. The destiny of notorious species is an impression of humankind's stewardship of planet, and the decisions today will decide the heritage left for people in the future.

CHAPTER 3

The Silent Cries

In the tremendous, interconnected embroidery of Earth's biological systems, there exists a significant and frequently neglected aspect — the quiet cries of endless species wavering near the precarious edge of elimination. These are the unheard supplications of animals whose presence is jeopardized by a heap of human-prompted dangers, from environment obliteration and environmental change to poaching and contamination. The quiet cries reverberation through the scenes and seas, resounding with the desperation of preservation, the delicacy of biodiversity, and the outcomes of humankind's activities on the fragile equilibrium of life.

In the core of Africa's immense savannahs and thick rainforests, the quiet cries of the African Elephant (Loxodonta africana) resound. These delicate goliaths, embellished with magnificent tusks and known for their complicated social designs, are wrestling with the ruthless attack of poaching for their ivory. The frightful quiet of elephants succumbing to unlawful hunting reverberations through the savannah, as their populaces decline abruptly. The quiet cries of these insightful creatures, whose presence originates before human development, are a supplication for their own endurance as well as a powerful call to mankind to rethink its relationship with nature.

In the Cold wild, the quiet cries of the polar bear (Ursus maritimus) reverberate across the softening ocean ice. These famous hunters, stunningly adjusted to the cruel polar climate, are confronting an existential danger because of environmental change. As ocean ice diminishes, polar bears battle to track down food, setting out on unsafe excursions looking for seals. The quiet of polar bears exploring an influencing world says a lot about the more extensive outcomes of an Earth-wide temperature boost. Their quiet cries highlight the interconnectedness of environments and the criticalness of relieving environmental change for all life on The planet.

The quiet cries of the magnificent Bengal Tiger (Panthera tigris) reverberation through the vanishing woodlands of the Indian subcontinent. Once unreservedly meandering tremendous scenes, these large felines currently battle with environment misfortune, poaching, and human-untamed life clashes. The frightful quiet of a decreased tiger populace signals the possible loss of an animal varieties as well as the disentangling of multifaceted biological connections. The quiet cries of Bengal Tigers challenge humankind to accommodate its growing impression with the basic to secure and safeguard the variety of life.

In the midst of the fog covered slants of Focal Africa's rainforests, the quiet cries of the mountain gorilla (Gorilla beringei) reverberate. This famous species, imparting a significant hereditary family relationship to people, faces dangers from environment misfortune, poaching, and illnesses communicated by people. The quiet of these delicate monsters, wrestling with the infringement of human exercises, addresses the more extensive difficulties of preservation in a time of fast ecological change. The quiet cries of mountain gorillas entice mankind to perceive its common obligation in protecting the mind boggling equilibrium of life.

In the high-elevation domains of Focal and South Asia, the quiet cries of the tricky snow panther (Panthera uncia) reverberation through the tough mountain scenes. Poaching, retaliatory killings, and territory fracture compromise the endurance of these superb hunters. The quiet cries of snow panthers, exploring a scene progressively formed by human exercises, act as a piercing wake up call of the delicacy of remarkable biological systems. Their situation urges humankind to reconsider its way to deal with coinciding with natural life and shielding the biodiversity of bumpy areas.

Underneath the waves, the quiet cries of the vaquita (Phocoena sinus), the world's littlest and generally imperiled cetacean, mumble in the Bay of California. With an expected populace in the simple twofold digits, the vaquita faces eradication fundamentally because of bycatch in unlawful gillnets. The frightful quietness of these minuscule porpoises highlights the interconnectedness of marine environments and the overwhelming effect of impractical fishing rehearses. The quiet cries of the vaquita resound as a critical advance notice about the results of ignoring the sensitive equilibrium of maritime life.

The quiet cries of the leatherback ocean turtle (Dermochelys coriacea) resound across tremendous maritime spans. As the biggest of all ocean turtle species, leatherbacks face dangers from environmental change, territory misfortune, and fisheries bycatch. The quiet of settling sea shores, once dynamic with the presence of these antiquated sailors, addresses the more extensive difficulties of marine preservation. The quiet cries of leatherback ocean turtles reverberation as a supplication to safeguard the imperativeness and flexibility of sea environments.

In the skies over, the quiet cries of the California condor (Gymnogyps californianus) wind through the tough scenes of North America. When near the precarious edge of annihilation because of lead harming and natural surroundings misfortune, these monster birds face continuous difficulties. The quiet of their wings rising above tremendous wild regions takes the stand concerning the intricacies of natural life recuperation and the constant dangers to imperiled species. The quiet cries of California condors reverberation as a sign of the flexibility of nature and the obligation mankind bears in molding what's to come.

The quiet cries of the meaningful ruler butterfly (Danaus plexippus) shudder across landmasses during their exceptional relocations. Natural surroundings misfortune, pesticide use, and environmental change undermine the mind boggling peculiarity of butterfly movement. The quietness of decreasing butterfly populaces flags a more extensive emergency in pollinator wellbeing and the sensitive dance among widely varied vegetation. The quiet cries of ruler butterflies resound as a supplication for the safeguarding of environments that rely upon their essential fertilization administrations.

The quiet cries of the Cross Stream gorilla (gorilla diehli) navigate the thick rainforests of Focal Africa. With a populace assessed at only two or three hundred people, these fundamentally jeopardized primates face living space misfortune and discontinuity because of farming and human settlement. The quietness of their decreasing populaces reverberations through the rainforest, moving mankind to accommodate its advancement desires with the basic to safeguard biodiversity. The quiet cries of the Cross Waterway gorilla call for reasonable land-use practices and global cooperation to get their future.

All in all, the quiet cries of these notorious species structure a tune that compasses across mainlands and biological systems. Their predicament is a dismal sign of the significant effect mankind has on the normal world and the ethical basic to go about as stewards of the planet. The quiet of these species talks not exclusively to their singular battles yet in addition to the more extensive difficulties of protection in a quickly impacting world. The quiet cries coax mankind to tune in, reflect, and answer with earnestness and empathy, for in their quiet supplications lies the destiny of biodiversity and the unpredictable snare of life that supports every one of us.

3.1 Examining the silent cries of endangered species and the threats they face.

In the tremendous span of Earth's environments, a piercing and frequently disregarded ensemble plays — the quiet cries of imperiled species wrestling with the impending danger of termination. These quiet cries reverberation through the complicated scenes, seas, and skies, uncovering the significant difficulties that these species go up against. Inspecting these quiet cries gives a window into the multi-layered dangers looked by imperiled species, revealing insight into the direness of preservation endeavors and the more extensive ramifications for the fragile equilibrium of our planet.

The unpleasant quiet of the African Elephant (Loxodonta africana) penetrates the savannahs and thick woodlands of Africa. Poaching for ivory, filled by unlawful natural life exchange, remains as an imposing danger to these delicate goliaths. The quiet cries of elephants, whose populaces are devastated for desired tusks, act as an obvious wake up call of the slippery human-driven powers pushing these grand animals towards the edge of presence. As elephants explore contracting environments and battle with the infringement of human exercises, their quiet cries coax mankind to address the main drivers of poaching, authorize hostile to poaching measures, and backer for global collaboration to defend their future.

In the cold Icy spreads, the quiet cries of the polar bear (Ursus maritimus) resonate as a chilling demonstration of the effects of environmental change. The quick downfall of ocean ice, an outcome of an Earth-wide temperature boost, represents an existential danger to these notorious hunters. The quiet cries of polar bears reverberation through the huge, softening scenes as they wrestle with the difficulties of tracking down food and adjusting to an evolving climate. Protection endeavors should address quick dangers as well as stand up to the more extensive issue of environmental change, highlighting the interconnectedness of biological systems and the critical requirement for worldwide drives to relieve ecological debasement.

The quiet cries of the Bengal Tiger (Panthera tigris) resonate through the decreasing timberlands of the Indian subcontinent. Natural surroundings misfortune, driven by human exercises like logging, horticulture, and urbanization, represents a desperate danger to these magnificent huge felines. The quiet cries of tigers reverberation as their domains shrivel, prompting expanded human-untamed life clashes and an elevated weakness to poaching. Preservation drives should focus on the security and reclamation of tiger environments, embracing an all encompassing methodology that includes neighborhood networks in economical land-use rehearses.

In the midst of the fog covered slants of Focal Africa's rainforests, the quiet cries of the mountain gorilla (Gorilla beringei) convey the heaviness of protection challenges. Living space obliteration, powered by horticulture and human settlement, represents an immediate danger to these delicate goliaths. The quiet cries of mountain gorillas resound as their regions shrivel, dividing populaces and restricting their capacity to flourish. Preservation endeavors should zero in on environment security, supportable land-use practices, and local area commitment to guarantee the endurance of these fundamentally imperiled primates.

In the high-elevation domains of Focal and South Asia, the quiet cries of the tricky snow panther (Panthera uncia) navigate the tough mountain scenes.

Poaching, retaliatory killings by herders, and natural surroundings fracture escalate the difficulties looked by these notorious huge felines. The quiet cries of snow panthers reverberation through the uneven territories as they explore a scene progressively molded by human exercises. Preservation drives should incorporate enemy of poaching measures, local area based protection programs, and manageable improvement procedures to get the eventual fate of these tricky hunters.

Underneath the waves, the quiet cries of the vaquita (Phocoena sinus) resound in the Bay of California. The vaquita, the world's littlest and generally imperiled cetacean, faces an existential danger because of bycatch in unlawful gillnets. The eerie quietness of these little porpoises highlights the pressing requirement for complete preservation measures to address unreasonable fishing rehearses and safeguard their marine territory. The quiet cries of the vaquita act as a piercing wake up call of the complicated interchange between marine life and human exercises, underlining the significance of feasible marine administration.

The quiet cries of the leatherback ocean turtle (Dermochelys coriacea) resound across immense maritime fields. Environmental change, territory misfortune, and fisheries bycatch present imposing difficulties to the endurance of these antiquated sailors. The quietness of settling sea shores, once dynamic with the presence of these monster turtles, addresses the more extensive emergency unfurling in marine environments. Preservation endeavors should incorporate the insurance of settling destinations, the decrease of plastic contamination, and the execution of turtle-accommodating fishing practices to address the multi-layered dangers looked by leatherback ocean turtles.

In the skies over, the quiet cries of the California condor (Gymnogyps californianus) wind through the tough scenes of North America. Lead harming, natural surroundings misfortune, and the persevering danger of microtrash ingestion have created a shaded area over the recuperation of these huge birds. The quietness of their wings rising above immense wild regions highlights the continuous difficulties looked by jeopardized species, even right after preservation triumphs. The quiet cries of California condors act as a call to intensify endeavors to address waiting dangers and guarantee the proceeded with recuperation of these notorious avian species.

The significant ruler butterfly (Danaus plexippus) conveys quiet cries across mainlands during its uncommon movements. Environment misfortune, pesticide use, and environmental change imperil the unpredictable peculiarity of butterfly movement. The quiet cries of decreasing butterfly populaces resonate through the scenes they cross, flagging a more extensive emergency in pollinator wellbeing and the sensitive harmony among widely varied vegetation. Preservation drives should focus on the security of rearing and overwintering territories, advance reasonable rural practices, and address the more extensive difficulties looked by pollinators.

The quiet cries of the Cross Waterway gorilla (gorilla diehli) navigate the thick rainforests of Focal Africa. With a populace assessed at only a couple hundred people, these fundamentally jeopardized primates face a daunting struggle against territory misfortune and fracture because of farming and human settlement. The quiet of their diminishing populaces reverberations through the rainforest, provoking humankind to accommodate its improvement goals with the basic to safeguard biodiversity. Preservation endeavors should incorporate reasonable land-use rehearses, local area commitment, and global coordinated effort to get the fate of these interesting primates.

Looking at the quiet cries of jeopardized species reveals a mind boggling embroidery of difficulties that stretch out a long ways past the singular situation of every species. The dangers looked by these famous animals mirror the more extensive issues of natural surroundings annihilation, environmental change, poaching, and impractical human exercises. The quiet cries entice humankind to tune in, comprehend, and act with desperation to address the main drivers of biodiversity misfortune. In the quietness of these species lies a significant call for aggregate liability, preservation development, and a recharged obligation to protecting the rich embroidery of life on The planet.

3.2 Discussion on habitat loss, poaching, climate change, and other factors contributing to their Decline.

The downfall of famous species, set apart by quiet cries that reverberation through their living spaces, is complicatedly woven into a story formed by a combination of anthropogenic powers. Looking at the diverse difficulties looked by these species uncovers a complicated exchange of natural surroundings misfortune, poaching, environmental change, and different elements that on the whole add to their hazardous downfall.

Territory misfortune arises as an essential impetus behind the quiet cries of imperiled species. Fast human extension, agrarian exercises, logging, and urbanization have all in all infringed upon the once-huge regions these species called home.

The African Elephant, for example, wanders savannahs and woodlands that are progressively divided by human settlements. As these environments recoil, so does the accessible space for these grand animals to scrounge, breed, and keep up with their mind boggling social designs. The quiet cries of elephants resound as the scenes they once explored unreservedly change into pockets of secluded and waning regions.

Additionally, the Bengal Tiger wrestles with lessening woods across the Indian subcontinent. As human requests for assets raise, perfect environments are supplanted by agribusiness and advancement, passing on tigers with limited spaces to meander. The quiet cries of tigers reverberation through divided scenes, moving their capacity to lay out and keep up with regions fundamental for their endurance. Preservation endeavors should address territory misfortune by advancing feasible land-use works on, making safeguarded regions, and drawing in with neighborhood networks to cultivate concurrence.

Environmental change arises as an impressive enemy in the battle for species endurance. The quiet cries of the polar bear reverberation through the softening Cold, a result of increasing worldwide temperatures. The sensational decrease of ocean ice disturbs the polar bear's capacity to chase after seals, their essential prey. The quiet cries of polar bears reverberate as they attempt unsafe excursions across tremendous stretches of vast water, driven by the need to track down food. Environmental change modifies the actual climate as well as stances flowing dangers to prey accessibility and, thus, the whole Icy biological system.

In precipitous locales, the quiet cries of the snow panther mix with the breezes that move throughout high-height scenes. Environmental change introduces shifts in vegetation, modifying the accessibility of prey for snow panthers. Increasing temperatures drive these tricky hunters to higher rises, getting their living spaces and carrying them into closer contact with human settlements. The quiet cries of snow panthers reverberate as they explore an evolving environment, a test that requires versatile preservation procedures to get their future in a warming world.

Poaching creates a long shaded area over the quiet cries of imperiled species, especially those with attractive assets. The frightful reverberation of discharges penetrates the once peaceful scenes possessed by the African Elephant. Poachers, driven by the illegal interest for ivory, devastate elephant populaces, abandoning a path of stranded calves and cracked social designs. The quiet cries of elephants act as an unfortunate wake up call of the continuous fight against poaching, underscoring the requirement for hearty enemy of poaching measures, policing, and global joint effort to destroy unlawful untamed life exchange organizations.

In the thick rainforests of Focal Africa, the quiet cries of the mountain gorilla entwine with the difficulties presented by poaching and natural surroundings debasement. These delicate monsters face dangers from the unlawful pet exchange and the infringement of human exercises. The quiet cries of mountain gorillas reverberation through districts where human-natural life struggle disturbs the fragile harmony among preservation and the vocations of nearby networks. Viable preservation procedures should address the underlying drivers of poaching, draw in networks in economical practices, and cultivate a common obligation to coincide with these imperiled primates.

Marine biological systems, as well, take the stand concerning the quiet cries of species, for example, the vaquita and leatherback ocean turtle, trapped by the outcomes of human exercises. The quiet cries of the vaquita reverberate in the Bay of California, trapped in unlawful gillnets set for the totoaba fish. The blow-back of bycatch sentences the vaquita extremely close to eradication. The quiet cries of leatherback ocean turtles reverberation across seas, where fisheries bycatch, plastic contamination, and beach front improvement risk their settling destinations and scavenging grounds. Tending to the decay of these species requests far reaching marine preservation procedures, global participation, and economical fisheries the executives.

Environmental change, territory misfortune, and poaching are exacerbated by a more extensive test — the overall effect of human exercises on the climate. The quiet cries of the California condor, once drove to the edge of eradication by lead harming from ingesting spent lead ammo, epitomize the complex connection between human activities and species decline. The quiet of these gigantic birds hovering over scenes set apart by lead defilement fills in as a call to redress the ecological results of human practices. Preservation drives should face the more extensive ecological impression of human exercises, pushing for reasonable works on, decreasing contamination, and encouraging concurrence with natural life.

The meaningful ruler butterfly, with its quiet cries carried on fragile wings, faces the complex danger of natural surroundings misfortune, pesticide use, and environmental change. The boundless utilization of herbicides and the change of normal natural surroundings into rural scenes reduce the accessibility of milkweed, a basic plant for ruler caterpillars. The quiet cries of ruler butterflies resound through diminishing populaces, testing the fragile dance between these pollinators and the environments they possess. Preservation endeavors should focus on the reclamation of ruler natural surroundings, advance reasonable farming, and address the foundational issues compromising pollinators.

The quiet cries of the Cross Stream gorilla navigate the rainforests of Focal Africa, where the difficulties of territory misfortune and discontinuity converge with the more extensive issue of impractical land-use rehearses. Horticulture, logging, and framework improvement add to the downfall of these fundamentally imperiled primates.

The quiet cries of Get Waterway gorillas reverberation through scenes where human advancement goals conflict with the basic to protect biodiversity. Preservation systems should draw in with nearby networks, advance economical land-use practices, and promoter for approaches that offset improvement with the assurance of regular natural surroundings.

In the assessment of living space misfortune, poaching, environmental change, and the more extensive effect of human exercises, a consistent idea arises — the dire requirement for complete and cooperative preservation endeavors. The quiet cries of imperiled species highlight the interconnectedness of biological systems, underlining that tending to a solitary danger is deficient.

Preservation techniques should be comprehensive, incorporating natural surroundings security, against poaching measures, environmental change relief, and local area commitment.

As humankind faces the results of its activities on the regular world, the quiet cries of imperiled species entice for a change in perspective — a shift towards a future where concurrence, maintainability, and biodiversity preservation are at the very front of worldwide needs. The quiet cries act as an impactful wake up call that the destiny of these notable species is entwined with the soundness of our planet, and in noticing their calls, we make a urgent stride towards a more agreeable and maintainable concurrence with the different life frames that offer Earth with us.

3.3 Stories of individual species and their struggles.

Inside the complex embroidery of Earth's environments, each jeopardized species recounts to a one of a kind and impactful story, a story of battle against a setting of living space misfortune, poaching, environmental change, and human infringement. These singular stories resound with the quiet cries of animals near the very edge of termination, meaningful of the more extensive difficulties looked by biodiversity.

In the core of the African savannahs, the African Elephant (Loxodonta africana) portrays a story of strength and weakness. With their superb tusks and perplexing familial bonds, these delicate monsters once meandered uninhibitedly across immense scenes. In any case, the reverberations of quiet cries resound as poaching for ivory devastates their populaces. The eerie accounts of elephants succumbing to hardhearted poachers highlight the pressing requirement for global joint effort to battle unlawful untamed life exchange, uphold hostile to poaching measures, and shield the environments that these notable animals call home.

In the thick rainforests of Focal Africa, the mountain gorilla (Gorilla beringei) winds around an account of connection and danger. These striking primates, sharing more than 98% of their DNA with people, face a dubious presence. The quiet cries of mountain gorillas reverberation through the fog covered inclines as living space misfortune and human infringement compromise their waning populaces.

Preservation endeavors center around laying out and keeping up with safeguarded regions, drawing in neighborhood networks in manageable practices, and moderating the effects of illnesses communicated by people. The account of the mountain gorilla represents the fragile harmony among mankind and the regular world.

High over the Cold Circle, the polar bear (Ursus maritimus) turns a story of endurance in a consistently evolving scene. With their notable white fur and strong casings, polar bears encapsulate the flexibility expected to explore the brutal Cold climate. Nonetheless, the quiet cries of polar bears reverberation through the liquefying ocean ice, a result of environmental change. As the ice withdraws, polar bears embrace deceptive excursions looking for lessening food sources. The account of polar bears highlights the critical requirement for worldwide environment activity to relieve the effects of increasing temperatures and save the frigid living spaces fundamental for their endurance.

In the thick backwoods of the Indian subcontinent, the Bengal Tiger (Panthera tigris) shares an account of covertness and weakness. When the undisputed leaders of tremendous regions, these magnificent enormous felines presently fight with the infringement of human exercises and the debasement of their natural surroundings. The quiet cries of Bengal Tigers reverberation through reducing woodlands, where the conflict among protection and improvement compromises their capacity to lay out regions and keep up with feasible populaces. Preservation drives wrestle with the intricacies of moderating human-untamed life clashes, implementing hostile to poaching measures, and advancing feasible land-use practices to get the fate of these notable hunters.

In the midst of the rough heaps of Focal and South Asia, the snow panther (Panthera uncia) epitomizes a story of secret and versatility. With their slippery nature and dazzling spotted coats, snow panthers explore the difficult territory of high-elevation scenes. In any case, their quiet cries resound as poaching, retaliatory killings by herders, and natural surroundings fracture strengthen. The tales of snow panthers highlight the requirement for local area based preservation endeavors, imaginative ways to deal with relieve human-untamed life clashes, and worldwide cooperation to safeguard these puzzling huge felines.

Underneath the waves in the Bay of California, the vaquita (Phocoena sinus) shares a story of covertness and weakness in the maritime profundities. The world's littlest and most jeopardized cetacean, the vaquita faces an up and coming danger of elimination because of bycatch in unlawful gillnets set for the totoaba fish. The quiet cries of the vaquita reverberation as progressives work vigorously to eliminate unlawful nets, authorize fishing guidelines, and make places of refuge to safeguard these little porpoises. The tale of the vaquita highlights the many-sided exchange between marine life and human exercises, accentuating the requirement for maintainable fisheries the board and global collaboration to shield the world's seas.

In the immense maritime spreads, the leatherback ocean turtle (Dermochelys coriacea) creates a story of old sailors and current difficulties. With their giant size and unmistakable calfskin like shells, these ocean turtles set out on legendary relocations across seas. Nonetheless, their quiet cries reverberation through settling sea shores undermined by environmental change, territory misfortune, and fisheries bycatch. Preservation drives endeavor to safeguard settling locales, diminish plastic contamination, and carry out turtle-accommodating fishing practices to guarantee the endurance of these antiquated sailors.

Over the skies of North America, the California condor (Gymnogyps californianus) portrays an account of close eradication and laborious recuperation. When near the precarious edge of vanishing totally, these goliath birds confronted lead harming from ingesting spent lead ammo. The quiet cries of California condors reverberate as protection endeavors, including hostage reproducing projects and lead ammo boycotts, pursue remaking their populaces. The narrative of the California condor fills in as a demonstration of the strength of nature and the basic of human mediation to redress the results of past activities.

On the wings of the breeze, the ruler butterfly (Danaus plexippus) conveys an account of unprecedented movements and delicate territories. With their dynamic orange and dark wings, ruler butterflies embrace a spectacular excursion across mainlands. Be that as it may, their quiet cries reverberation through scenes where environment misfortune, pesticide use, and environmental change undermine the many-sided peculiarity of butterfly movement. Protection drives center around reestablishing milkweed living spaces, advancing supportable horticulture, and bringing issues to light about the essential job of pollinators in environments.

In the rainforests of Focal Africa, the Cross Waterway gorilla (gorilla diehli) shares a story of segregation and weakness. With a populace assessed at only a couple hundred people, these fundamentally jeopardized primates face territory misfortune and fracture because of horticulture and human settlement. The quiet cries of Get Stream gorillas resound through the rainforest, moving humankind to accommodate advancement yearnings with the basic to protect biodiversity. Protection endeavors focus on reasonable land-use rehearses, local area commitment, and global joint effort to get the fate of these novel primates.

Every one of these accounts, told by individual species, adds to the more extensive story of biodiversity in danger. The quiet cries of these animals reverberation through their territories, filling in as an impactful sign of the dire requirement for protection activity. The difficulties looked by these species are not detached occurrences but rather interconnected strings in the perplexing trap of life on The planet. Their stories propel mankind to tune in, comprehend, and act all in all to save the rich woven artwork of biodiversity that supports every one of us.

CHAPTER 4

The Conservation Crusade

The Preservation Campaign is a complex development that has advanced over the course of the years to address the squeezing natural difficulties confronting our planet. This campaign is powered by an aggregate feeling of obligation to save and safeguard the World's sensitive biological systems, biodiversity, and normal assets. As we dig into the different features of this protection exertion, it becomes clear that it isn't simply a mission yet a significant reaction to the raising dangers presented by human exercises and environmental change.

At the core of the Preservation Campaign lies the acknowledgment that the World's biological systems are interconnected, and the prosperity of one is unpredictably connected to the prosperity of all. This interconnectedness frames the establishment for the all encompassing methodology that characterizes the protection development. The crusaders, including researchers, preservationists, policymakers, and concerned residents, endeavor to address the main drivers of natural corruption while at the same time executing useful answers for alleviate its effects.

One of the critical mainstays of the Protection Campaign is the safeguarding of biodiversity. Earth is home to an unbelievable cluster of plant and creature species, each assuming a one of a kind part in keeping up with environmental equilibrium. In any case, the disturbing pace of species termination represents a critical danger to this biodiversity. Traditionalists work eagerly to distinguish imperiled species, safeguard their territories, and carry out methodologies to guarantee their endurance. The objective isn't just to protect individual species however to save the perplexing trap of connections that supports life on our planet.

Living space obliteration arises as a significant milestone in the Preservation Campaign. Quick urbanization, deforestation, and modern extension have prompted the debasement and fracture of essential biological systems. Traditionalists advocate for the foundation of safeguarded regions, public parks, and untamed life stores to give places of refuge to imperiled species. Besides, they stress the significance of reasonable land-use practices to work out some kind of harmony between human turn of events and ecological protection.

Environmental change stands apart as an impressive enemy in the Protection Campaign. The consuming of non-renewable energy sources, deforestation, and modern exercises add to the ascent in ozone depleting substance outflows, prompting a dangerous atmospheric devation and eccentric weather conditions. Traditionalists perceive the desperation of moderating environmental change and elevating transformation systems to limit its effect on weak biological systems and networks. Environmentally friendly power, afforestation, and feasible agrarian practices are vital parts of the preservation weapons store in the battle against environmental change.

Instruction and mindfulness structure the bedrock of the Preservation Campaign. Enabling people with information about the significance of ecological preservation encourages a feeling of stewardship for the planet. Traditionalists participate in open effort programs, natural training drives, and backing efforts to prepare networks and gather support for protection arrangements. By imparting a feeling of obligation and ecological morals, the campaign expects to make a worldwide development where each individual turns into a proactive member in the mission for a practical future.

The Preservation Campaign expands its impact into the domains of strategy and administration. Backing for powerful ecological approaches, severe guidelines, and global collaboration is vital for impact significant change. Preservationists team up with state run administrations, NGOs, and worldwide associations to shape arrangements that focus on ecological insurance, economical turn of events, and the evenhanded circulation of assets. The preservation plan rises above borders, underlining the requirement for a brought together worldwide work to address the common difficulties confronting mankind.

Even with exceptional difficulties, innovation arises as an important partner in the Protection Campaign. Advancements, for example, satellite observing, information investigation, and man-made reasoning add to the assortment and examination of urgent natural information. This data helps protectionists in going with informed choices, distinguishing preservation needs, and observing the viability of mediations. Innovation likewise works with public commitment through web-based stages, empowering a more extensive crowd to partake in protection endeavors and add to resident science drives.

Local area inclusion is a foundation of the Preservation Campaign. Perceiving the personal association between nearby networks and their surroundings, preservationists team up with native people groups and customary networks to incorporate conventional information and practices into protection systems. This comprehensive methodology reinforces the versatility of environments as well as regards the privileges and goals of neighborhood networks. By encouraging a feeling of pride and shared liability, the Protection Campaign endeavors to make economical arrangements that benefit both nature and individuals.

Challenges, nonetheless, have large amounts of the Protection Campaign. Monetary interests, political struggles, and contending needs frequently present snags to the execution of compelling protection measures. Finding some kind of harmony among protection and advancement requires exploring complex financial elements and arranging compromises that guarantee the drawn out soundness of the planet. The crusaders face the overwhelming errand of beating protection from change and encouraging an aggregate obligation to a feasible future.

The Protection Campaign is certainly not a static undertaking yet a dynamic and developing development that adjusts to new difficulties and valuable open doors. As logical information progresses and our comprehension of environments develops, preservation procedures are refined and extended. The crusaders perceive the requirement for consistent learning and advancement to remain in front of arising dangers and to foster reasonable arrangements that endure over the extreme long haul.

All in all, the Protection Campaign addresses an aggregate and decided work to defend the World's normal legacy for people in the future. A source of inspiration rises above individual interests and public limits, stressing the common obligation of mankind to be stewards of the planet. As we explore the intricacies of the cutting edge world, the Preservation Campaign fills in as an encouraging sign, moving us to reevaluate our relationship with nature and work towards an amicable concurrence that guarantees the prosperity of every living being and the life span of our valuable planet.

4.1 Profiles of dedicated conservationists and organizations on the front lines.

Devoted moderates and associations on the forefronts of the ecological fight assume a vital part in safeguarding the World's biodiversity and regular assets. These people and gatherings are driven by an enthusiasm for nature, a profound feeling of obligation, and a promise to having a substantial effect. Their profiles give understanding into the assorted methodologies and procedures utilized in the continuous Preservation Campaign.

Dr. Jane Goodall:

Perhaps of the most notable figure in the domain of protection is Dr. Jane Goodall, a primatologist, ethologist, and anthropologist. Her historic work with chimpanzees in Gombe Stream Public Park in Tanzania upset how we might interpret these canny and social animals. Dr. Goodall's devotion to untamed life protection stretches out past her logical commitments; she established the Jane Goodall Foundation in 1977, which centers around local area based preservation and ecological schooling. The foundation's inventive projects expect to safeguard natural surroundings, advance manageable jobs for neighborhood networks, and motivate the up and coming age of ecological stewards. Dr. Goodall's eager support for creatures and the climate has acquired her various honors, and she stays a compelling voice in the worldwide preservation development.

David Attenborough:

Sir David Attenborough, a famous telecaster and normal student of history, has turned into a worldwide minister for ecological preservation through his narratives that feature the magnificence of the regular world and the critical need to safeguard it. With a profession traversing many years, Attenborough's unmistakable voice and narrating ability have brought the miracles of nature into front rooms all over the planet. His narratives, for example, "Planet Earth" and "Blue Planet," grandstand the World's fantastic biodiversity as well as revealed insight into the dangers it faces. Past his on-screen commitments, Attenborough has been a promoter for environment activity and preservation strategies. His capacity to associate with crowds and convey the significance of protecting the planet has made him a vital figure in the Preservation Campaign.

World Natural life Asset (WWF):

On the hierarchical front, the World Natural life Asset (WWF) stands apart as a worldwide power in natural life protection. Established in 1961, WWF works in more than 100 nations and is committed to safeguarding the world's most weak species and environments.

The association utilizes a science-based way to deal with protection, dealing with the ground to defend territories, battle unlawful natural life exchange, and address the underlying drivers of ecological corruption. WWF additionally participates in backing and strategy drives, asking state run administrations and organizations to embrace reasonable practices. Teaming up with neighborhood networks, legislatures, and different NGOs, WWF represents the significance of worldwide collaboration in handling complex protection challenges.

Greenpeace:

As an unmistakable ecological non-legislative association (NGO), Greenpeace has been at the front of worldwide natural missions since its foundation in 1971. Known for its immediate activity approach, Greenpeace crusades on a great many issues, including deforestation, overfishing, environmental change, and contamination. The association's notorious fights and inventive backing strategies catch public consideration and push for foundational change. Greenpeace's obligation to defying natural dangers head-on has made it a main impetus in the Protection Campaign, moving legislatures and enterprises to focus on supportability and environmental obligation.

Leakey Establishment:

Established by paleoanthropologist Louis Leakey in 1968, the Leakey Establishment centers around understanding human development and supporting exploration that adds to how we might interpret the normal world. While its essential spotlight is on paleoanthropology, the establishment perceives the interconnectedness of human development and the more extensive biological system. By putting resources into research allows, the Leakey Establishment upholds researchers concentrating on primates, biological systems, and the effect of ecological changes on biodiversity. The establishment's work highlights the significance of investigating our developmental history to illuminate preservation techniques for what's to come.

Rainforest Establishment:

The Rainforest Establishment, laid out in 1989 by performer Sting and his better half Trudie Styler, is committed to safeguarding the world's rainforests and the privileges of native people groups who call these backwoods home. The association centers around grassroots drives that engage neighborhood networks, perceiving the fundamental job native individuals play in protecting biodiversity. Through land privileges backing, feasible improvement ventures, and associations with nearby associations, the Rainforest Establishment attempts to battle deforestation and advance preservation that regards both the climate and the social legacy of native networks.

Paul Rancher - Accomplices In Wellbeing:

While not customarily connected with protection, Paul Rancher and his association, Accomplices In Wellbeing (PIH), epitomize the interconnectedness of natural and human prosperity. PIH, established in 1987, works in devastated networks all over the planet, giving medical care, fortifying medical care frameworks, and tending to the social determinants of wellbeing. Rancher's work accentuates the effect of ecological variables on general wellbeing, featuring what environmental change and natural corruption excessively mean for weak populaces. By tending to wellbeing variations and the underlying drivers of illness, Accomplices In Wellbeing in a roundabout way adds to the more extensive objectives of the Preservation Campaign by advancing flexibility in networks confronting ecological difficulties.

Untamed life Preservation Society (WCS):

The Untamed life Preservation Society, laid out in 1895, brags a rich history protection accomplishments. Working in excess of 60 nations, WCS oversees untamed life saves, conducts logical examination, and executes preservation programs that length earthbound and marine biological systems. The association's all encompassing methodology consolidates on-the-ground preservation endeavors, logical exploration, and local area commitment to safeguard imperiled species and their territories. WCS additionally focuses on tending to the main drivers of natural life decline, including poaching, territory misfortune, and environmental change. By incorporating science with reasonable preservation arrangements, the Untamed life Protection Society represents the far reaching and cooperative nature of compelling protection endeavors.

These profiles offer a brief look into the different scene of devoted progressives and associations driving the charge in the Preservation Campaign. From spearheading researchers like Jane Goodall to powerful telecasters like David Attenborough, and from worldwide NGOs like WWF and Greenpeace to establishments like the Leakey Establishment and the Rainforest Establishment, every element offers a one of a kind point of view and set of systems that would be useful.

The Preservation Campaign, as exemplified by these people and associations, is a dynamic and cooperative exertion that perceives the criticalness of tending to ecological difficulties while upholding for an agreeable conjunction among mankind and the normal world. Through their aggregate undertakings, these traditionalists and associations move trust and show that positive change is feasible when enthusiasm, science, and promotion combine chasing a manageable future.

4.2 Showcasing successful conservation initiatives and strategies.

Effective protection drives and procedures act as encouraging signs in the continuous fight to safeguard our planet's biodiversity and normal assets. As the worldwide local area wrestles with ecological difficulties, these drives show that with devotion, advancement, and joint effort, accomplishing significant and enduring protection outcomes is conceivable. Looking at a scope of examples of overcoming adversity gives significant bits of knowledge into the different methodologies that have demonstrated successful in safeguarding environments, imperiled species, and the sensitive equilibrium of our planet.

1. **Costa Rica's Spearheading Protection Model:**
   Costa Rica stands apart as a brilliant illustration of fruitful preservation through its spearheading way to deal with safeguarded regions and supportable turn of events. In the twentieth 100 years, Costa Rica confronted broad deforestation because of logging and agrarian development. Nonetheless, during the 1980s, the public authority carried out a strong preservation procedure that zeroed in on laying out public stops and holds. Today, almost a fourth of Costa Rica's property is safeguarded, encouraging biodiversity and supporting ecotourism. This imaginative model has not just added to the recuperation of numerous species yet has additionally supported the nation's economy, showing the similarity of protection and maintainable turn of events.

2. **The Yellowstone Wolves Renewed introduction:**
   The renewed introduction of wolves to Yellowstone Public Park in the US in 1995 is a milestone preservation example of overcoming adversity. Wolves, which had been missing from the recreation area for almost 70 years, were once again introduced to control the expanding elk populace, which was causing overgrazing and adversely affecting vegetation. The

wolves' return significantly affected the whole biological system. As the wolves went after elk, the number of inhabitants in deer, the essential prey of elk, expanded. This prompted changes in vegetation, emphatically affecting different species like beavers and larks. The Yellowstone Wolves Renewed introduction embodies the idea of trophic fountains, exhibiting how the renewed introduction of a cornerstone animal categories can affect a whole environment.

3. **The Incomparable Green Wall Drive:**
   The Incomparable Green Wall is an aggressive skillet African drive pointed toward fighting desertification, land debasement, and environmental change. Sent off in 2007, the venture imagines a mosaic of green and useful scenes across the Sahel locale, extending from Senegal to Djibouti.

   By establishing a belt of dry season safe trees and vegetation, the drive looks to reestablish corrupted land, give vocations to neighborhood networks, and relieve the effects of environmental change. The Incomparable Green Wall epitomizes the soul of global collaboration, with different African nations, the African Association, and different accomplices cooperating to address ecological difficulties and work on the strength of weak biological systems.

4. **The Galápagos Islands' Intrusive Species Destruction:**
   The Galápagos Islands, famous for their one of a kind biodiversity and the motivation they gave to Charles Darwin's hypothesis of development, confronted an extreme danger from intrusive species. Non-local species presented by human exercises, like rodents, goats, and intrusive plants, were unleashing destruction on the islands' fragile biological systems. Accordingly, the Galápagos Public Park sent off aggressive destruction programs, effectively dispensing with obtrusive species from a few islands. The evacuation of intrusive species has permitted local vegetation to recuperate, giving basic territory to endemic species. The Galápagos Islands' preservation achievement exhibits the significance of proactive measures to control and kill obtrusive species to safeguard weak biological systems.

5. **The Installment for Environment Administrations (PES) Approach:**
   The Installment for Biological system Administrations (PES) approach has gotten momentum as an inventive procedure to boost preservation by doling out worth to the environmental administrations given by regular environments. This idea includes remunerating landowners or networks for keeping up with or reestablishing environment administrations like clean water, carbon sequestration, and biodiversity preservation. In Costa Rica, the public authority executed a fruitful PES program, where landowners get installments for saving woodlands that add to watershed

security. The PES approach adjusts monetary motivations to protection objectives, cultivating an economical connection between human exercises and the common habitat.

6. **Local area Based Protection in Namibia:**
Namibia's people group based protection model has exhibited the adequacy of including nearby networks in untamed life the executives and preservation. Despite poaching dangers and clashes among untamed life and nearby populaces, Namibia carried out common conservancies, where neighborhood networks are given the power and motivating forces to oversee natural life and advantage from protection endeavors. This approach has prompted an exceptional recuperation of untamed life populaces, including imperiled species like dark rhinos. By incorporating the interests of neighborhood networks with preservation objectives, Namibia's people group based protection model features the potential for mutual benefit arrangements that advance both manageable turn of events and biodiversity preservation.

7. **The Marine Safeguarded Regions (MPAs) Organization:**
The foundation of Marine Safeguarded Regions (MPAs) all over the planet has arisen as a critical technique to shield marine environments and biodiversity. These regions, where human exercises are limited or controlled, give asylum to marine species, support fisheries, and upgrade generally speaking environment wellbeing. Models like the Chagos Marine Save in the Indian Sea and the Papahānaumokuākea Marine Public Landmark in the Pacific exhibit the effect of enormous scope marine protection endeavors. The MPAs network underscores the interconnectedness of sea biological systems and the significance of worldwide cooperation in tending to the difficulties looked by marine conditions.

8. **Rewilding Drives:**
Rewilding, the most common way of reestablishing and safeguarding normal environments while once again introducing or safeguarding local species, has acquired noticeable quality as a protection system. The renewed introduction of cornerstone species and the reclamation of normal cycles can extraordinarily affect environments. The Oostvaardersplassen in the Netherlands is a great representation of a rewilding example of overcoming adversity, where the making of a wetland environment prompted the unconstrained colonization of different plant and creature species. Rewilding drives feature the strength of environments when permitted to recuperate and the potential for huge scope reclamation endeavors to turn around biological debasement.

9. **The Save the Elephants Lobby in Kenya:**
The Save the Elephants lobby in Kenya, drove by associations like Save the Elephants and the Elephant Emergency Asset, represents fruitful

endeavors to address the poaching emergency and safeguard imperiled species. Through people group commitment, hostile to poaching drives, and mechanical developments, for example, GPS following collars, progressives have figured out how to diminish elephant poaching and secure basic territories. The mission highlights the significance of tending to both the interest for ivory and the main drivers of poaching, while additionally featuring the job of neighborhood networks in safeguarding notorious species.

10. **Supportable Fisheries The executives:**

The shift towards supportable fisheries the executives has turned into a basic part of worldwide protection endeavors, particularly given the danger of overfishing to marine biological systems. Drives like the Marine Stewardship Gathering (MSC) confirmation program set guidelines for reasonable fishing works on, guaranteeing that fisheries comply to rules that advance long haul ecological wellbeing.

By empowering capable fishing practices and purchaser mindfulness, maintainable fisheries the board looks to adjust the requirements of human populaces subject to fisheries with the basic to save marine biodiversity.

All in all, the displayed effective protection drives and procedures epitomize the variety of approaches and the potential for positive change in the domain of ecological conservation. Whether through creative arrangements like Costa Rica's safeguarded regions, local area commitment as found in Namibia's conservancies, or worldwide cooperation exemplified by the Incomparable Green Wall, these examples of overcoming adversity feature the significance of versatility and joint effort.

The Preservation Campaign, as exhibited by these drives, requires multilayered arrangements that address the perplexing difficulties confronting our planet. By gaining from these triumphs and expanding upon them, the worldwide local area can keep pursuing a manageable future where the sensitive equilibrium of nature is safeguarded for a long time into the future.

4.3 Examining the challenges and triumphs in the fight against extinction.

Looking at the difficulties and wins in the battle against termination gives a nuanced point of view on the complex and frequently dubious condition of biodiversity protection. The battle to forestall the irreversible loss of species traverses a range of obstructions, from anthropogenic exercises to environmental irregular characteristics. In any case, in the midst of these difficulties, there have been outstanding victories and procedures that deal expect the eventual fate of imperiled species and their environments.

Challenges in the Battle Against Eradication:

1. **Natural surroundings Misfortune and Fracture:**
   One of the essential difficulties in the battle against termination is territory misfortune and discontinuity. Human exercises, like deforestation, urbanization, and rural development, have essentially adjusted and diminished regular territories, passing on species with restricted space to flourish. Discontinuity further worsens the issue, secluding populaces and ruining hereditary variety. The infringement of human improvement into basic natural surroundings frequently disturbs the sensitive equilibrium of biological systems, driving species to the edge of eradication.

2. **Environmental Change:**
   The phantom of environmental change poses a potential threat over protection endeavors, representing a complex danger to biodiversity. Climbing temperatures, adjusted precipitation examples, and outrageous climate occasions disturb biological systems, affecting the appropriation and conduct of species. Environmental change compounds existing stressors, making it more moving for species to adjust. Polar bears battling with softening ice covers and coral reefs surrendering to blanching occasions are powerful instances of the significant effect environmental change has on weak species.

3. **Overexploitation and Poaching:**
   Overexploitation, driven by the interest for assets like lumber, untamed life items, and intriguing pets, represents a huge danger to numerous species. Poaching, powered by the unlawful exchange natural life, targets notable species like elephants, rhinos, and tigers. The financial motivations related with these exercises frequently lead to the consumption of populaces and the interruption of environments. Progressives wrestle with the troublesome errand of authorizing guidelines and battling coordinated wrongdoing networks participated in the illegal natural life exchange.

4. **Obtrusive Species:**
   The acquaintance of obtrusive species with new conditions upsets laid out biological connections, frequently with destroying results. Obtrusive plants, creatures, and microorganisms can outcompete local species, go after them, or present infections for which the local species need invulnerability. The effects of obtrusive species echo through biological systems, adjusting supplement cycles and environment elements. Islands, specifically, are vulnerable to the unfavorable impacts of obtrusive species, prompting the decay of endemic verdure.

5. **Contamination:**

Contamination, in different structures, represents an unavoidable danger to both earthbound and oceanic biological systems. Synthetic contaminations, plastic waste, and impurities from modern exercises corrupt environments and damage natural life. The presentation of contaminations into water bodies influences sea-going life, prompting decreases in fish populaces and undermining species reliant upon freshwater environments. Addressing contamination requires coordinated endeavors to direct businesses, advance reasonable practices, and bring issues to light about the results of contamination on biodiversity.

Wins in the Battle Against Termination:

1. **Species Recuperation Projects:**
   Species recuperation programs, frequently including hostage reproducing and renewed introduction endeavors, have been instrumental in bringing specific species back from the edge of termination. The California condor, for example, confronted a critical circumstance with just 27 people staying in the wild during the 1980s. Through escalated hostage reproducing and preservation endeavors, the populace has expanded, and there are currently more than 400 condors, with some effectively once again introduced into their normal living space. Comparable examples of overcoming adversity incorporate the dark footed ferret and the red wolf, the two of which were safeguarded from the edge of termination through committed rearing projects.

2. **Preservation Holds and Safeguarded Regions:**
   The foundation of preservation holds and safeguarded regions assumes a urgent part in giving places of refuge to imperiled species. These regions, going from public parks to untamed life asylums, offer insurance from natural surroundings annihilation, poaching, and other anthropogenic tensions. The renewed introduction of wolves to Yellowstone Public Park and the recuperation of the dim whale populace are instances of how safeguarded regions can add to the resurgence of species and the reclamation of biological systems.

3. **Global Collaboration and Arrangements:**
   Global collaboration through arrangements and shows has demonstrated viable in tending to transboundary preservation issues. The Show on Worldwide Exchange Imperiled Types of Wild Fauna and Verdure (Refers to), for example, directs the global exchange of jeopardized species and their parts. The Antarctic Arrangement and the Show on Organic Variety are different instances of worldwide endeavors to defend environments and forestall the eradication of species. These arrangements highlight the significance of cooperative ways to deal with protection that rise above public boundaries.

4. **Local area Based Protection Drives:**
Enabling nearby networks to effectively partake in preservation endeavors has demonstrated to be a fruitful methodology. As a rule, native networks have customary information that can add to compelling preservation rehearses. Local area based protection drives, for example, those in Namibia where neighborhood networks oversee conservancies, show that when individuals are straightforwardly associated with preservation direction, it prompts more feasible results. Adjusting the requirements of neighborhood networks with preservation objectives is urgent for the drawn out progress of these drives.

5. **Progresses in Innovation and Exploration:**
Mechanical headways and logical examination have altogether improved preservation endeavors. GPS following, satellite symbolism, and information investigation give significant instruments to checking untamed life populaces, concentrating on movement designs, and recognizing basic natural surroundings. Protection hereditary strategies assist with evaluating hereditary variety and guide rearing projects. These mechanical apparatuses not just guide in that frame of mind of species elements yet in addition add to the improvement of focused on and successful preservation procedures.

6. **Public Mindfulness and Training:**

Raising public mindfulness and encouraging a feeling of natural stewardship are vital to effective protection. Instructive drives, narratives, and effort programs assist with building public help for preservation endeavors and impact customer conduct. The worldwide development against single-use plastics, for instance, has picked up speed because of expanded familiarity with its effect on marine life. Public strain and support assume a fundamental part in considering legislatures and companies responsible for their effect on biodiversity.

Incorporated Approaches:
The difficulties and wins in the battle against eradication highlight the significance of coordinated and all encompassing ways to deal with preservation. A complete technique should address the underlying drivers of biodiversity misfortune while utilizing the victories accomplished through designated intercessions. Coordinated protection approaches perceive the interconnectedness of environmental, social, and monetary variables, going for the gold advantage both natural life and human networks.

1. **Feasible Improvement Objectives (SDGs):**
The Unified Countries' Feasible Improvement Objectives (SDGs) give a system to tending to worldwide difficulties, including those connected with

biodiversity and environments. Objective 15 explicitly centers around life ashore, underscoring the significance of safeguarding, reestablishing, and advancing manageable utilization of earthbound environments. Accomplishing the SDGs requires a cooperative and interdisciplinary methodology that thinks about the relationship of ecological, social, and monetary elements.

2. **Environment Based Protection:**
Environment based protection approaches focus on the wellbeing and strength of whole biological systems as opposed to zeroing in exclusively on individual species.

By safeguarding and reestablishing biological systems, traditionalists address the basic variables adding to species decline. The idea of rewilding, which includes reestablishing normal cycles and once again introducing cornerstone species, lines up with this biological system based approach. Environment flexibility is essential for the drawn out endurance of species in their regular territories.

3. **Versatile Administration Techniques:**
Preservation procedures should be versatile and receptive to evolving conditions. Versatile administration includes continuous checking, appraisal, and change of protection mediations in view of new data and arising difficulties. This approach recognizes the unique idea of environments and the requirement for adaptable systems that can advance over the long run. Versatile administration is especially vital even with vulnerabilities connected with environmental change and other worldwide stressors.

4. **Coordinated effort Between Partners:**
Coordinated effort between states, non-legislative associations (NGOs), neighborhood networks, and the confidential area is fundamental for viable preservation. The contribution of different partners guarantees a more far reaching comprehension of the difficulties and potential open doors related with preservation drives. Public-private organizations, as seen in corporate-supported protection projects, can give assets and mastery to supplement legislative and non-benefit endeavors.

5. **Preservation Money and Motivators:**

Creating maintainable subsidizing systems for preservation is urgent for the drawn out progress of drives. Preservation finance includes utilizing monetary assets from different areas, including charity, influence money management, and ecotourism. Installment for Environment Administrations (PES) programs, where landowners get remuneration for keeping up with biological administrations, gives monetary impetuses to protection. By adjusting financial interests to preservation objectives, these drives make a more supportable model for safeguarding biodiversity.

All in all, analyzing the difficulties and wins in the battle against eradication features the complex idea of preservation endeavors. While various snags persevere, from living space misfortune to environmental change, achievements in species recuperation, safeguarded region the board, and worldwide coordinated effort offer beams of trust. The way ahead requires a promise to coordinated and versatile methodologies that perceive the interconnectedness of environmental, social, and monetary frameworks. By gaining from both the difficulties and wins, the worldwide local area can take a stab at a more supportable future where the rich embroidery of life on Earth is saved for a long time into the future.

CHAPTER 5

Urgent Calls for Action

Pressing calls for activity resonate across the globe as mankind wrestles with a heap of interconnected emergencies that compromise the actual texture of our reality. From the raising environment crisis to biodiversity misfortune, ecological corruption, social treacheries, and worldwide wellbeing dangers, the requirement for quick and groundbreaking activity is more squeezing than any other time in recent memory. These dire calls radiate from researchers, activists, networks, and concerned residents who perceive the desperation of addressing these difficulties to get a feasible and fair future for all.

1. **Environment Emergency:**
   At the front of pressing calls for activity is the environment emergency, a worldwide crisis driven by the steady expansion in ozone depleting substance outflows. The Intergovernmental Board on Environmental Change (IPCC) gives distinct alerts about the irreversible effects of a worldwide temperature alteration, including rising ocean levels, outrageous climate occasions, and interruptions to biological systems. Critical activity is basic to restrict worldwide temperature increments to 1.5 degrees Celsius above pre-modern levels, an edge past which the results become disastrous. Calls for progressing to environmentally friendly power sources, decreasing fossil fuel byproducts, and carrying out supportable practices are fundamental to moderate the effects of environmental change and construct a versatile future.

2. **Biodiversity Misfortune:**
   The disturbing pace of biodiversity misfortune is another dire concern requesting prompt consideration. Species elimination, territory obliteration, and the corruption of biological systems compromise the fragile equilibrium of the normal world. The Worldwide Appraisal Report on Biodiversity and Biological system Administrations, distributed by the

Intergovernmental Science-Strategy Stage on Biodiversity and Environment Administrations (IPBES), features the interconnectedness of biodiversity, human prosperity, and the strength of the planet. Pressing calls for activity accentuate the requirement for preservation endeavors, reasonable land-use rehearses, and the security of basic living spaces to save biodiversity and forestall irreversible harm to biological systems.

3. **Ecological Corruption:**
The corruption of the climate incorporates a scope of interconnected issues, including deforestation, contamination, soil disintegration, and loss of arable land. Earnest calls for activity stress the significance of embracing economical practices across areas, from farming to industry. Tending to ecological corruption requires rethinking utilization designs, advancing round economies, and embracing innovations that limit natural effect. The corruption of normal assets is unpredictably connected to social and monetary disparities, making pressing activity basic for cultivating an amicable connection among mankind and the climate.

4. **Civil rights and Value:**
Calls for critical activity reach out past natural worries to incorporate civil rights and value. The effects of environmental change and natural debasement excessively influence minimized networks, intensifying existing imbalances. Native populaces, specifically, endure the worst part of natural shameful acts, from the infringement on their territories to the disturbance of customary lifestyles. Earnest activity in the domain of civil rights includes perceiving and amending verifiable treacheries, enhancing the voices of minimized networks, and executing arrangements that focus on value and inclusivity even with natural difficulties.

5. **Worldwide Wellbeing:**
Worldwide wellbeing emergencies, embodied by occasions like the Coronavirus pandemic, highlight the interconnectedness of human wellbeing and the strength of the planet. Critical calls for activity in the domain of worldwide wellbeing underline the requirement for hearty medical services frameworks, impartial admittance to immunizations and therapies, and readiness for future pandemics. The One Wellbeing approach, perceiving the reliance of human, creature, and natural wellbeing, is key to tending to arising irresistible sicknesses and protecting the prosperity of the two biological systems and networks.

6. **Feasible Improvement Objectives (SDGs):**
The Unified Countries Feasible Improvement Objectives (SDGs) act as a complete system for pressing activity across different fronts. From killing neediness to guaranteeing clean water, quality schooling, orientation uniformity, and environment activity, the SDGs frame a guide for accomplishing a practical and fair world by 2030. Calls for earnest activity

community on adjusting arrangements, ventures, and aggregate endeavors with the SDGs to address the complex and interlinked difficulties confronting mankind.

7. **Corporate Obligation:**
   Pressing calls for activity stretch out to the corporate area, with an accentuation on corporate obligation and manageability. Organizations, as significant supporters of natural debasement, are encouraged to take on harmless to the ecosystem rehearses, lessen their carbon impression, and embrace social obligation. The idea of Natural, Social, and Administration (ESG) measures is acquiring noticeable quality, empowering organizations to think about the more extensive effects of their procedure on the climate and society. Calls for supportable strategic approaches highlight the job of the confidential area in driving positive change and adjusting monetary exercises to the critical requirement for natural and social stewardship.

8. **Sustainable power Progress:**
   A crucial part of pressing activity spins around progressing from petroleum derivatives to environmentally friendly power sources. The consuming of petroleum derivatives is an essential driver of environmental change, and critical calls for activity underline the basic to move to feasible and clean energy choices. The fast organization of sun based, wind, and other inexhaustible innovations is fundamental to diminish reliance on petroleum products, decline fossil fuel byproducts, and encourage a progress towards a more practical energy scene.

9. **Roundabout Economy and Waste Decrease:**
   The straight model of utilization, described by "take, make, arrange," adds to natural corruption and asset consumption. Earnest calls for activity advocate for the reception of a round economy, where assets are reused, reused, and reused. Limiting waste, advancing reasonable creation and utilization examples, and embracing round economy standards are vital for moderating the natural effect of human exercises.

10. **Preservation of Water Assets:**

Water shortage and contamination present huge dangers to biological systems and human prosperity. Earnest calls for activity in water preservation highlight the requirement for dependable water the executives, security of watersheds, and tending to contamination in streams, lakes, and seas. Reasonable horticulture rehearses, water reusing, and the safeguarding of freshwater environments are essential parts of dire endeavors to guarantee the accessibility of clean water for ebb and flow and people in the future.

All in all, earnest calls for activity reverberate across a range of interconnected difficulties confronting humankind. From the existential danger of the environment emergency to the complex trap of biodiversity misfortune, natural debasement, social treacheries, and worldwide wellbeing emergencies, the requirement for quick and extraordinary activity is clear.

The desperation isn't only a clarion call for transform; it is an aggregate affirmation of the obligation every person, local area, government, and business bears in shielding the planet and guaranteeing an economical and impartial future. The viability of this pressing activity lies in its quickness as well as in the cooperative and all encompassing methodology taken to address the complex and interlinked difficulties that characterize our time. Just through purposeful and supported endeavors might humankind at any point desire to explore the way towards a strong, evenhanded, and feasible future for a long time into the future.

5.1 Exploring the role of advocacy in raising awareness.

Investigating the job of backing in bringing issues to light enlightens the force of aggregate voices in resolving basic issues, from civil rights to natural protection. Support fills in as an impetus for change, utilizing correspondence, training, and preparation to bring issues to light and rouse activity. This diverse methodology includes people, associations, and networks meeting up to enhance key messages, challenge standards, and encourage a feeling of obligation toward shared difficulties. Looking at the complexities of promotion discloses its extraordinary likely in molding general assessment, impacting strategies, and making a groundswell of help for issues that request consideration.

1. **Characterizing Support:**

   At its center, support includes the coordinated work to impact leaders, arrangements, and general sentiments on unambiguous issues. Advocates champion makes going from common liberties and civil rights natural supportability and general wellbeing. The objective isn't just to bring issues to light yet in addition to achieve substantial change by impacting perspectives, ways of behaving, and arrangements.

   Promotion works on numerous levels, incorporating grassroots developments, non-administrative associations (NGOs), and even people who utilize their foundation to support makes close their hearts.

2. **Molding Public Discernment:**

   Promotion assumes a critical part in molding public discernment by scattering data, testing misguided judgments, and outlining issues in a way that reverberates with different crowds. By utilizing narrating, convincing stories, and drawing in happy, supporters can adapt complex issues and make them engaging to individuals' lives. This close to home association is much of the time a strong impetus for bringing issues to light, as it prompts people to understand the difficulties looked by others and urges them to make a move.

3. **Assembling Grassroots Developments:**
One of the most powerful parts of promotion is its capacity to prepare grassroots developments, where people meet up to advocate for change at the nearby level. Grassroots support enables networks to resolve gives that straightforwardly influence them, cultivating a feeling of organization and aggregate liability. Whether it's upholding for civil rights, natural insurance, or medical care change, grassroots developments frequently act as the main impetus behind more extensive cultural movements.

4. **Ecological Support:**
In the domain of ecological preservation, backing assumes a critical part in resolving major problems, for example, environmental change, deforestation, and biodiversity misfortune. Natural promoters bring issues to light about the effects of human exercises in the world, stressing the desperation of embracing supportable practices. Through crusades, instructive drives, and strategy support, natural backers endeavor to impact popular assessment and drive fundamental changes that advance biological stewardship.

5. **Common freedoms and Civil rights Promotion:**
Support is a key part in the battle for common liberties and civil rights. It fills in as an amazing asset to challenge foundational imbalances, segregation, and treacheries. Developments like People of color Matter, LGBTQ+ freedoms support, and missions against orientation based brutality embody the groundbreaking effect of backing in bringing issues to light about issues connected with equity and equity. Advocates shed light on foundational issues as well as activate networks to request change and responsibility.

6. **Instruction and Mindfulness Missions:**
Training and mindfulness crusades are vital parts of support systems. Whether led through conventional media, online entertainment, or local area exceed, these missions mean to illuminate general society about unambiguous issues, scatter fantasies, and give significant data. Advocates utilize different mediums, including narratives, web-based entertainment stages, and public occasions, to contact assorted crowds and encourage informed conversations around basic themes.

7. **Strategy Promotion:**
Promotion broadens its impact into the domain of policymaking, where backers work to shape regulation and government strategies that address cultural difficulties. Campaigning, key correspondence, and alliance building are normal apparatuses in strategy promotion. By drawing in with legislators, pushing for explicit authoritative changes, and preparing

public help, advocates add to the definition of approaches that mirror the requirements and upsides of the networks they address.

8. **Impacting Corporate Practices:**
Backing additionally reaches out to affecting corporate practices, particularly with respect to issues connected with moral strategic approaches, natural obligation, and social effect. Advocates frequently target partnerships through crusades that shed light on deceptive practices, energize straightforwardness, and request responsibility. By utilizing customer pressure, media consideration, and investor support, activists look to achieve positive changes in corporate way of behaving.

9. **Enhancing Underrepresented Voices:**
A center standard of support is enhancing the voices of the people who might be minimized or underrepresented. Advocates work to guarantee that the points of view and worries of weak networks are heard and tended to. This inclusivity is basic in cultivating a more impartial society and resolving foundational issues that lopsidedly influence specific gatherings.

10. **Challenges in Promotion:**
Regardless of its extraordinary potential, backing faces various difficulties. Incredulity, falsehood, and the polarization of public talk can ruin the viability of support endeavors. Moreover, backers might experience obstruction from those with contradicting sees or settled in interests. Exploring these difficulties requires vital correspondence, truth based informing, and a pledge to encouraging discourse that extensions separates.

11. **The Job of Web-based Entertainment:**
In the computerized age, web-based entertainment has arisen as a useful asset for promotion, empowering backers to contact worldwide crowds and prepare support quickly. Hashtag developments, online missions, and advanced narrating give roads to people to share their encounters, express fortitude, and make energy for social and ecological causes. Web-based entertainment stages act as powerful spaces for exchange, data scattering, and the association of virtual and genuine occasions.

12. **Support in Emergency Reaction:**
Backing takes on elevated importance in the midst of emergency, whether catastrophic events, pandemics, or helpful crises. Advocates assume a vital part in bringing issues to light about the effect of emergencies, preparing assets for aid ventures, and considering specialists responsible for powerful reaction and recuperation. In such circumstances, backing fills in as a life saver for impacted networks, guaranteeing that their requirements are met and their voices are heard in the midst of the disorder.

13. **The Interconnection of Support:**
Support frequently works at the crossing point of various issues,

perceiving the interconnectedness of social, ecological, and monetary difficulties. The idea of multifacetedness recognizes that people and networks experience a conversion of persecutions and treacheries. Viable support embraces a multifaceted methodology, tending to the intricacies of covering frameworks of separation and pursuing complete arrangements that think about the variety of human encounters.

14. **Estimating the Effect of Backing:**
Evaluating the effect of backing endeavors is a perplexing errand, as the results are many times diverse and long haul. Measurements, for example, changes in general assessment, strategy changes, expanded mindfulness, and unmistakable upgrades in networks are signs of support achievement. Promotion associations frequently utilize a blend of quantitative and subjective techniques, including reviews, media examination, and contextual investigations, to gauge the viability of their missions.

15. **The Eventual fate of Support:**

As the world wrestles with continuous and arising difficulties, the job of support is ready to advance. The rising interconnectedness of worldwide issues, the ascent of computerized advancements, and the basic for aggregate activity highlight the proceeded with pertinence of backing in molding what's in store.

The crossing point of promotion with arising fields like man-made consciousness, bioethics, and reasonable improvement proclaims new outskirts for supporters to investigate as they look for inventive answers for complex issues.

All in all, investigating the job of support in bringing issues to light uncovers its importance as an impetus for change across a range of issues. From natural preservation to basic liberties, promotion fills in as a strong power for molding general assessment, impacting strategies, and preparing networks. The extraordinary capability of backing lies in its capacity to enhance voices, rock the boat, and encourage an aggregate feeling of obligation for the prosperity of the planet and its occupants. As we explore the difficulties of the present and future, promotion remains as an encouraging sign, moving people and networks to effectively participate chasing an all the more, feasible, and even-handed world.

5.2 Discussion on the importance of public involvement and policy changes.
A complete conversation on the significance of public contribution and strategy changes highlights the key job that connected with residents play in molding the course of administration and strategy making. The communication between general society and the strategies that oversee them is a powerful cycle, wherein the voices, concerns, and goals of individuals add to the turn of events and refinement of strategies. This conversation dives into the meaning

of public contribution in the strategy making process, the systems through which residents can partake, and the extraordinary effect that all around educated and drew in networks can have on arrangement changes.

1. **Majority rule Establishment:**
   At the core of the significance of public association in strategy changes lies the primary standard of a vote based system. In equitable social orders, the authenticity of administration comes from the assent and cooperation of the represented. Public contribution guarantees that strategies are not forced for arbitrary reasons yet are intelligent of the aggregate will and needs of individuals. Basically, a majority rule framework blossoms with the dynamic commitment of residents in forming the strategies that influence their lives.

2. **Informed Navigation:**
   Public contribution in strategy changes works with informed direction. By drawing in with general society, policymakers get to different viewpoints, master experiences, and a complete comprehension of the nuanced main things. Residents bring certifiable encounters and limited information that advance the approach making process. Informed choices, established in the real factors of those straightforwardly impacted, can possibly yield more viable and impartial strategies.

3. **Guaranteeing Portrayal:**
   Public inclusion is significant for guaranteeing that strategy changes are illustrative of the different socioeconomics and interests inside a general public. It forestalls the minimization of specific gatherings and guarantees that the advantages and weights of approaches are disseminated impartially. The consideration of underrepresented voices in the dynamic cycle advances civil rights and encourages a feeling of inclusivity in administration.

4. **Building Trust and Authenticity:**
   Drawing in the general population in the arrangement making process encourages trust and authenticity in government activities. At the point when residents feel that their feedback is esteemed and thought of, it improves their confidence in the public authority's capacity to address their interests. This trust is fundamental for keeping up with social attachment and guaranteeing the soundness of vote based organizations. Conversely, strategies created without public contribution can prompt distrust, opposition, and a deficiency of trust in legislative direction.

5. **Local area Strengthening:**
   Public contribution enables networks by providing them with a feeling of organization and responsibility for strategies that influence their lives. At the point when people and networks effectively take part in molding

choices, they become partners in the results. This strengthening can prompt expanded metro commitment, local area union, and a common obligation to the benefit of everyone. Enabled people group are bound to play a functioning job in carrying out and supporting approaches over the long haul.

6. **Further developed Approach Viability:**
Public association adds to the viability of approaches by taking advantage of the aggregate insight of the populace. It furnishes policymakers with significant bits of knowledge into the likely effects and potentially negative results of proposed measures. Through open meeting, experimental runs projects, and criticism components, policymakers can refine and change arrangements to guarantee they are benevolent as well as down to earth and successful in accomplishing their planned results.

7. **Responsive Administration:**
Public contribution makes a responsive and versatile administration structure. Social orders develop, and the necessities of the public change after some time.

Ordinary commitment with residents permits policymakers to remain receptive to moving needs, arising difficulties, and advancing assumptions. This responsiveness is pivotal for keeping up with the importance and adequacy of strategies in unique and quickly evolving conditions.

8. **Components of Public Contribution:**
Different components exist to work with public association in the approach making process. Conventional structures incorporate formal proceedings, official Q&A events, and resident warning sheets. Present day innovation has extended these roads through internet based gatherings, online entertainment stages, and advanced studies. These components guarantee that public inclusion isn't restricted by geological requirements and can arrive at a different and wide range of the populace.

9. **Government funded Training and Mindfulness:**
A fundamental part of compelling public association is schooling and mindfulness. Guaranteeing that residents approach precise data about arrangement issues empowers informed cooperation. States and support bunches assume a pivotal part in dispersing data, cultivating municipal proficiency, and making stages for discourse. Informed residents are better prepared to contribute seriously to strategy conversations and backer for changes lined up with their qualities.

10. **Strategy Changes and Social Developments:**
By and large, the absolute most critical strategy changes have been catalyzed by friendly developments that electrifies public inclusion. Developments pushing for social equality, natural security, orientation correspondence, and other social issues play had a critical impact in molding

strategies and impacting official changes. The aggregate force of connected residents, coordinated under a typical reason, can possibly achieve extraordinary strategy shifts.

11. **Support and Campaigning:**

Past direct open inclusion, promotion gatherings and campaigning endeavors act as persuasive channels through which residents can shape approaches. These associations work to address explicit interests, enhance specific voices, and impact leaders. While some censure the job of campaigning in strategy transforms, it stays a real method through which residents can guarantee their interests are heard at the most elevated levels of government.

12. **Worldwide Viewpoints:**

The significance of public contribution in approach changes isn't restricted to individual countries. The worldwide idea of many difficulties, including environmental change, general wellbeing emergencies, and common liberties issues, requires global cooperation.

Worldwide residents, through backing, mindfulness missions, and support in global discussions, add to forming strategies that address transnational difficulties and maintain shared values.

13. **Beating Difficulties to Public Contribution:**

Notwithstanding its benefits, public inclusion faces difficulties, including issues of availability, inconsistent portrayal, and the impact of personal stakes. Conquering these difficulties requires purposeful endeavors to make comprehensive stages, address abberations in admittance to data, and carry out measures to neutralize the unbalanced impact of strong elements. Finding some kind of harmony that guarantees wide and significant cooperation is a continuous undertaking in fortifying vote based administration.

14. **Contextual analyses in Effective Public Association:**

Analyzing contextual investigations of fruitful public association gives experiences into the substantial effect residents can have on arrangement changes. The social liberties development in the US, the counter politically-sanctioned racial segregation development in South Africa, and later models like the worldwide environment strikes drove by youth activists feature how public contribution can drive fundamental change and impact strategy choices.

15. **Mechanical Headways and Future Patterns:**

Progressions in innovation keep on reshaping the scene of public association. From online stages for public counsels to blockchain advances that improve straightforwardness, the computerized period presents new open doors and difficulties.

Future patterns might see expanded utilization of man-made consciousness in breaking down open information, computer generated reality for vivid city commitment, and decentralized advancements that engage residents in phenomenal ways.All in all, the significance of public association in approach changes is characteristic for the majority rule administration system. It guarantees that strategies are established in the necessities and desires of individuals they influence.

Through informed independent direction, portrayal, and strengthening, public association adds to the authenticity and viability of approaches. As social orders wrestle with complex difficulties, the continuous obligation to encouraging significant public contribution stays fundamental to making approaches that truly serve the benefit of all and mirror the common upsides of different networks.

5.3 Encouraging a collective response to the urgent calls for action.

Empowering an aggregate reaction to pressing calls for activity is a basic in tending to the complex difficulties that mankind faces. From environmental change and biodiversity misfortune to social shameful acts and worldwide wellbeing emergencies, the interconnected idea of these issues requires co-operative endeavors at nearby, public, and worldwide levels. This conversation investigates the significance of encouraging an aggregate reaction, the key components that add to its prosperity, and the job of people, networks, legislatures, and worldwide coordinated effort in affecting significant change.

1. **Perceiving Interconnected Difficulties:**
   The direness of aggregate activity originates from the acknowledgment that a considerable lot of the difficulties confronting this present reality are interconnected and frequently intensify each other. For example, the effects of environmental change have expansive outcomes on biological systems, human wellbeing, and social solidness. Recognizing these interconnections is fundamental for creating comprehensive and compelling arrangements that address the underlying drivers of perplexing issues.

2. **Worldwide Nature of Difficulties:**
   Numerous contemporary difficulties rise above public lines, requiring an organized reaction on a worldwide scale. The Coronavirus pandemic distinctively represents how a wellbeing emergency can immediately turn into a worldwide test, influencing social orders, economies, and medical care frameworks around the world. Despite such worldwide difficulties, the call for aggregate activity becomes an ethical basic as well as a down to earth need for defending the prosperity of humankind in general.

3. **Shared Liability:**
Empowering an aggregate reaction highlights the common obligation that people, networks, states, and associations bear in resolving earnest issues. This common obligation includes perceiving that everybody plays a part to play, and aggregate endeavors are expected to impact significant change. Whether it's diminishing fossil fuel byproducts, advancing civil rights, or fighting the spread of irresistible sicknesses, the feeling of shared liability cultivates a cooperative soul.

4. **Grassroots Developments:**
One of the main impetuses behind an aggregate reaction is the force of grassroots developments. These developments frequently arise naturally from networks, filled by energetic people who prepare others around a typical reason. Models incorporate youth-drove environment strikes, local area driven preservation endeavors, and civil rights developments. Grassroots developments bring issues to light as well as make a groundswell of help that comes down on organizations and catalyzes bigger scope changes.

5. **Enabling People group:**
An aggregate reaction is best when it enables networks to take responsibility for challenges they face. Engaged people group are stronger and versatile, fit for creating inventive arrangements that suit their one of a kind settings. This strengthening includes furnishing networks with the assets, information, and office to effectively take part in dynamic cycles and carry out maintainable arrangements.

6. **Comprehensive Direction:**
Empowering an aggregate reaction requires comprehensive dynamic cycles that esteem different viewpoints and encounters. Consideration guarantees that the voices of minimized and weak networks are heard, and their exceptional requirements are viewed as in approach definition. Comprehensive dynamic encourages a feeling of responsibility and responsibility among different partners, prompting more maintainable and impartial results.

7. **Administrative Authority:**
Legislatures assume a vital part in empowering an aggregate reaction by giving administration, establishing strategies, and designating assets. Solid and serious administrative initiative is urgent for setting the plan, laying out administrative structures, and driving fundamental changes. States can go about as impetuses for aggregate activity by cultivating joint effort between different areas, carrying out proof based strategies, and advancing public commitment.

8. **Worldwide Collaboration:**
Many difficulties, especially those connected with the climate, general

wellbeing, and basic liberties, require worldwide participation. Empowering an aggregate reaction at the worldwide level includes fashioning organizations between countries, global associations, and non-legislative substances. Worldwide joint effort works with the trading of information, assets, and best works on, making a brought together front against difficulties that rise above public limits.

9. **Utilizing Innovation:**
Progressions in innovation assume a urgent part in empowering an aggregate reaction by working with correspondence, cooperation, and data spread. Web-based entertainment stages, online discussions, and advanced apparatuses give roads to people and networks to associate, share data, and coordinate aggregate activities. Innovation likewise empowers the fast assembly of assets and backing during emergencies, intensifying the effect of aggregate endeavors.

10. **Schooling and Mindfulness:**
An aggregate reaction is dependent upon far and wide instruction and mindfulness about the earnestness of the difficulties within reach. Instruction enables people with information, encouraging a more profound comprehension of the issues and their suggestions. Mindfulness crusades, whether directed by states, non-benefit associations, or grassroots developments, illuminate general society, motivate activity, and make a feeling of shared liability.

11. **Corporate Social Obligation:**
Notwithstanding legislatures, organizations and partnerships assume a significant part in empowering an aggregate reaction. Corporate social obligation (CSR) includes organizations coordinating moral, social, and natural contemplations into their activities. By adjusting strategic policies to supportability objectives, enterprises add to the more extensive aggregate exertion and show the way that monetary thriving can coincide with social and ecological obligation.

12. **Logical Coordinated effort:**
Logical joint effort is vital in tending to complex difficulties that require interdisciplinary methodologies and particular information. Empowering an aggregate reaction includes encouraging joint effort among researchers, specialists, and specialists from different fields. This coordinated effort upgrades the comprehension of complicated issues, speeds up the advancement of arrangements, and guarantees that strategies depend on sound logical proof.

13. **Adjusting Individual and Aggregate Activity:**
While an aggregate reaction is fundamental, perceiving the job of individual action is similarly significant. Empowering people to embrace economical practices, settle on naturally cognizant decisions, and take

part in city exercises adds to the aggregate exertion. Adjusting individual and aggregate activity makes a synergistic impact, where limited scope changes at the singular level add to bigger foundational shifts.

14. **Versatile Administration Designs:**

An aggregate reaction requires versatile administration structures that can answer changing conditions and integrate criticism from different partners. Administration models that underscore adaptability, straightforwardness, and responsibility are better prepared to explore complex difficulties. These designs cultivate cooperation between government bodies, common society, and confidential elements, empowering a more durable and facilitated approach.

15. **Beating Boundaries to Aggregate Activity:**

Empowering an aggregate reaction frequently faces obstructions like political opposition, personal stakes, and fundamental idleness. Defeating these hindrances requires key methodologies that include building coalitions, utilizing public strain, and tending to the underlying drivers of opposition. Viable correspondence, featuring shared advantages, and underlining the drawn out results of inaction are fundamental parts of conquering hindrances to aggregate activity.

All in all, reassuring an aggregate reaction to dire calls for activity is a basic for tending to the interconnected difficulties confronting humankind. The co-operative endeavors of people, networks, legislatures, and global elements are fundamental for making significant and practical arrangements. By cultivating a feeling of shared liability, enabling networks, and utilizing innovation and logical coordinated effort, an aggregate reaction can catalyze extraordinary change and fabricate a stronger, impartial, and economical future for a long time into the future.

CHAPTER 6

Biodiversity's Silent Quake

Biodiversity, frequently alluded to as Earth's quiet spine, is going through a quiet shudder of extraordinary greatness, with significant ramifications for the planet's wellbeing and the fate of life on The planet. This quiet shudder is set apart by the speeding up loss of biodiversity, driven by human exercises, for example, environment obliteration, contamination, environmental change, and over-double-dealing of regular assets. As the mind boggling snare of life disentangles, the repercussions stretch out a long ways past the domains of environment, influencing biological systems, economies, and human prosperity. This talk dives into the different components of biodiversity misfortune, its underlying drivers, natural results, and the pressing requirement for a deliberate worldwide reaction to moderate its sweeping impacts.

1. **The Orchestra of Life:**
   Biodiversity incorporates the amazing assortment of life structures on The planet, from minute organic entities to transcending trees, and from the profundities of the seas to the most elevated mountain tops. This orchestra of life, containing a great many animal types, assumes a basic part in keeping up with the equilibrium and versatility of environments. Biodiversity isn't simply a theoretical idea however a dynamic and interconnected force that supports life-supporting cycles, like fertilization, supplement cycling, and the guideline of environment.

2. **Speeding up Loss of Biodiversity:**
   The quiet shudder grasping biodiversity is appeared in the speeding up loss of species at a remarkable rate. Researchers depict the flow period as the Anthropocene, an age set apart by human strength and impact on Earth's frameworks. The eradication rate is assessed to be 100 to multiple times higher than the normal foundation rate, prompting a rush

of terminations practically identical to the mass elimination occasions in Earth's land history.

3. **Main drivers of Biodiversity Misfortune:**
Human exercises stand as the essential drivers behind the quiet tremor of biodiversity misfortune. Natural surroundings obliteration through exercises like deforestation and urbanization adjusts environments, leaving species without appropriate homes. Contamination, whether from synthetics, plastics, or different foreign substances, corrupts living spaces and stances direct dangers to different species. Environmental change, filled by the consuming of petroleum products, modifies temperature and precipitation designs, disturbing biological systems and pushing species past their endurance limits. Over-abuse of natural life for food, medication, and exchange further speeds up biodiversity decline.

4. **Natural Outcomes:**
The repercussions of biodiversity misfortune reach out across environments and have flowing impacts on natural capabilities. The deficiency of pollinators, like honey bees and butterflies, compromises food security by risking the multiplication of various plants that people depend on for food. Decreases in cornerstone species, which assume lopsidedly enormous parts in their environments, can prompt the unwinding of whole food networks. Biodiversity misfortune additionally debilitates the capacity of biological systems to endure natural shocks, making them more helpless against infection flare-ups, obtrusive species, and environment limits.

5. **Monetary Ramifications:**
Biodiversity misfortune isn't bound to the domain of environment; it has broad monetary ramifications. Numerous people group rely straightforwardly upon biodiversity for their vocations, whether through horticulture, fisheries, or ranger service. The deficiency of biodiversity can disturb these ventures, prompting monetary difficulties for those dependent on regular assets. Moreover, the debasement of biological systems reduces their ability to offer essential types of assistance, for example, water sanitization, flood control, and environment guideline, putting extra monetary weights on social orders.

6. **Human Prosperity and Wellbeing:**
The quiet tremor of biodiversity misfortune likewise compromises human prosperity and wellbeing in manners that are frequently underrated. Biodiversity is a wellspring of different food varieties, including natural products, vegetables, and creature items. The hereditary variety inside species is critical for reproducing crops that are versatile to nuisances, sicknesses, and changing natural circumstances. Medications got from plants and creatures are basic to medical care, and the deficiency of biodiversity lessens the pool of likely drug assets.

7. **Social and Moral Aspects:**
Biodiversity holds colossal social and moral importance for human social orders. Native societies, specifically, have profound associations with their normal environmental elements, seeing biodiversity not simply as assets yet as substances with inherent worth and social significance. The deficiency of species and environments compromises conventional information frameworks and disintegrates the social texture of networks that have existed together with nature for ages.

8. **Tipping Focuses and Irreversible Changes:**
The quiet shudder of biodiversity misfortune raises worries about arriving at basic tipping focuses, past which environments might go through irreversible changes. These tipping focuses could bring about sudden and devastating shifts, for example, the breakdown of whole environments or the deficiency of key biological system administrations. The trepidation is that once these tipping focuses are crossed, the capacity of environments to recuperate and recover might be seriously compromised.

9. **Preservation Endeavors and Safeguarded Regions:**
Endeavors to alleviate biodiversity misfortune frequently include laying out safeguarded regions to defend basic environments and carrying out protection measures. Safeguarded regions, going from public parks to marine stores, act as sanctuaries for jeopardized species and biodiversity areas of interest. In any case, difficulties like deficient financing, lacking implementation, and the infringement of human exercises present critical obstacles to the adequacy of preservation endeavors.

10. **Reclamation and Reforestation:**
Past security, reclamation endeavors assume a pivotal part in fighting biodiversity misfortune. Reforestation projects, wetland reclamation, and natural surroundings restoration add to the recuperation of environments and give valuable chances to dislodged species to restore populaces.
These drives, frequently determined by a mix of legislative, non-administrative, and local area endeavors, intend to invert the harm caused for biological systems and advance the recuperation of biodiversity.

11. **Maintainable Advancement Objectives (SDGs):**
The Unified Countries' Manageable Improvement Objectives (SDGs) perceive the significance of biodiversity and incorporate targets connected with its preservation and practical use. Objective 15 explicitly centers around securing, reestablishing, and advancing practical utilization of earthly biological systems, fighting desertification, and stopping biodiversity misfortune. Coordinating biodiversity contemplations into more extensive improvement plans is vital for accomplishing maintainable results across monetary, social, and natural aspects.

12. **Individual and Aggregate Activity:**
    Tending to the quiet shudder of biodiversity misfortune requires both individual and aggregate activity. People can contribute by taking on economical ways of life, supporting preservation drives, and pushing for strategies that focus on biodiversity. Aggregate activity includes cooperative endeavors at nearby, public, and worldwide levels. Legislatures, organizations, and common society associations should cooperate to create and execute strategies that offset human improvement with the conservation of biodiversity.

13. **Worldwide Arrangements and Shows:**
    Worldwide collaboration is principal notwithstanding a worldwide quiet shudder. Shows and arrangements, like the Show on Organic Variety (CBD), give structures to nations to team up on biodiversity protection. The CBD's Aichi Targets and, all the more as of late, the Post-2020 Worldwide Biodiversity System put forth aggressive objectives to stop biodiversity misfortune and advance the manageable utilization of regular assets.

14. **Training and Mindfulness:**
    Schooling and mindfulness crusades assume an essential part in cultivating a more profound comprehension of biodiversity and its significance. Ecological training, from school educational plans to public effort programs, adds to building a feeling of obligation and stewardship towards nature. Expanded mindfulness can prompt informed decisions and motivate people to partake in biodiversity preservation endeavors effectively.

15. **The Job of Innovation:**

Innovation, including remote detecting, information examination, and hereditary exploration, adds to checking biodiversity, grasping environment elements, and illuminating protection procedures. Propels in biotechnology offer open doors for imaginative methodologies, for example, hereditary preservation and engineered science to moderate the effect of biodiversity misfortune. Nonetheless, moral contemplations and cautious assessment of potential dangers are fundamental in sending these advancements.

All in all, the quiet shudder of biodiversity misfortune represents a significant danger to the actual underpinning of life on The planet. Its repercussions reach out from biological interruptions to financial difficulties, affecting human prosperity and social legacy. Relieving this quiet shake requires a comprehensive methodology that incorporates preservation endeavors, manageable improvement practices, and worldwide joint effort. The desperation of the circumstance requests an aggregate reaction from people, networks, states, and the worldwide local area to protect the variety of life and secure a reasonable future for a long time into the future.

6.1 Delving into the broader impact of species loss on ecosystems.

Diving into the more extensive effect of species misfortune on environments reveals a mind boggling trap of interdependencies and results that resonate all through biological frameworks. The deficiency of species, driven by human exercises, for example, natural surroundings annihilation, contamination, environmental change, and over-double-dealing, upsets the sensitive equilibrium of biological systems. This conversation investigates the flowing impacts of species misfortune on biodiversity, environment capabilities, strength, and the general security of regular frameworks.

1. **Biodiversity as the Texture of Environments:**
   Biodiversity is the texture that winds around environments together, containing an immense range of animal types communicating in multifaceted ways. Every species, whether huge or little, assumes an extraordinary part in keeping up with the wellbeing and usefulness of its environment. The variety of living things guarantees that biological systems are strong, versatile, and fit for answering ecological changes.

2. **Cornerstone Species and Trophic Fountains:**
   Certain species, known as cornerstone species, generally affect their biological systems. The evacuation of a cornerstone animal types can set off trophic fountains, where the impacts echo through various levels of the natural pecking order. For instance, the downfall of hunters can prompt an overpopulation of their prey, which, thus, influences vegetation and modifies the whole environment structure.

3. **Pollinators and Conceptive Achievement:**
   The downfall of pollinators, like honey bees and butterflies, addresses a basic part of animal groups misfortune with broad results. Many plants depend on these pollinators for proliferation through the exchange of dust between blossoms. The deficiency of pollinators upsets this cycle, undermining the conceptive progress of various plant species, including those that give fundamental food assets to people.

4. **Biological system Security and Protection from Annoyances:**
   Biodiversity adds to the solidness and strength of environments. Various biological systems are better prepared to endure and recuperate from aggravations, whether they be regular occasions like out of control fires or human-incited tensions like contamination. Species-rich biological systems frequently show more elevated levels of protection from irritations, illnesses, and obtrusive species, making them stronger notwithstanding natural difficulties.

5. **Hereditary Variety and Versatility:**
   Inside species, hereditary variety is vital for flexibility and endurance. Populaces with different hereditary pools have a more prominent ability

to answer changing ecological circumstances, remembering shifts for temperature, precipitation, or the predominance of infections. Hereditary variety guarantees that species can develop over the long haul, upgrading their capacity to adapt to arising dangers.

6. **Supplement Cycling and Disintegration:**
Numerous species, especially microorganisms, parasites, and bugs, assume fundamental parts in supplement cycling and decay. Decomposers separate natural matter, delivering supplements once more into the dirt for plants to utilize. The deficiency of decomposer species upsets this cycle, prompting awkward nature in supplement accessibility and influencing the general efficiency of environments.

7. **Biological system Administrations and Human Prosperity:**
Biological systems give many administrations fundamental for human prosperity. These biological system administrations incorporate clean water, air decontamination, fertilization of yields, and guideline of environment. Species misfortune sabotages the limit of biological systems to convey these administrations, presenting direct dangers to human well-being, agribusiness, and the general personal satisfaction.

8. **Natural surroundings Designing and Biological system Specialists:**
A few animal types, frequently alluded to as biological system designers, shape and change their natural surroundings, making conditions helpful for the endurance of different species. For example, beavers fabricate dams that make wetland natural surroundings, helping different plants, creatures, and microorganisms. The vanishing of such natural surroundings designing species can have flowing impacts on whole environments.

9. **Trophic Levels and Energy Stream:**
Environments are organized into trophic levels, addressing various situations in the well established pecking order. Each trophic level is reliant upon the one beneath it for energy move. The deficiency of species at any trophic level upsets the progression of energy through the biological system, influencing the overflow and circulation of different species inside the food web.

10. **Natural Versatility and Environment Guideline:**
Biodiversity adds to natural versatility, characterized as the limit of environments to retain and recuperate from unsettling influences. Flawless environments, with different species gatherings, assume a pivotal part in environment guideline by sequestering carbon and impacting neighborhood weather conditions. Species misfortune compromises these administrative capabilities, worsening the effects of environmental change.

11. **Social and Stylish Qualities:**
Biological systems hold social and tasteful qualities that go past their utilitarian capabilities. The variety of vegetation adds to the magnificence

of regular scenes and has propelled imaginative, otherworldly, and sporting encounters for human social orders from the beginning of time. The deficiency of species reduces these social and stylish qualities, dissolving the association among individuals and the normal world.

12. **Natural surroundings Discontinuity and Detachment:**
Human exercises, like urbanization and foundation improvement, lead to territory fracture, detaching populaces of species. Divided natural surroundings limit the development of species, lessening hereditary trade and expanding the weakness of detached populaces to nearby eliminations. This fracture further speeds up species misfortune and debilitates environment elements.

13. **Obtrusive Species and Changed Environment Elements:**
The presentation of obtrusive species, frequently worked with by human exercises, represents a huge danger to local biodiversity. Obtrusive species can outcompete local species for assets, present new infections, and disturb laid out environmental connections. The subsequent changes in biological system elements can prompt the downfall or relocation of local species, worsening the effects of biodiversity misfortune.

14. **Overfishing and Marine Environments:**
Overfishing, driven by the interest for fish, represents an extreme danger to marine biodiversity. The consumption of fish stocks upsets marine biological systems, influencing the harmony among hunter and prey species. The deficiency of key species in marine environments, for example, sharks or cornerstone species like ocean otters, can set off far and wide natural lopsided characteristics with repercussions for fisheries and waterfront networks.

15. **Preservation Methodologies and Rebuilding Endeavors:**

Alleviating the more extensive effect of species misfortune on biological systems requires complete protection procedures and rebuilding endeavors. Preservation endeavors center around safeguarding basic living spaces, executing feasible asset the executives rehearses, and tending to the main drivers of biodiversity misfortune.

Reclamation drives include reforestation, territory recovery, and renewed introduction programs pointed toward revamping populaces of jeopardized species.All in all, diving into the more extensive effect of species misfortune on environments discloses the multifaceted embroidered artwork of interdependencies that portray the regular world. The quiet tremor of biodiversity misfortune has significant ramifications for the steadiness, flexibility, and usefulness of environments.

Perceiving the worth of biodiversity and executing proactive preservation measures are essential moves toward alleviating these effects and saving the multifaceted equilibrium that supports life on The planet. As mankind explores the difficulties of the Anthropocene, an aggregate obligation to biodiversity preservation becomes principal for the prosperity of environments, human social orders, and the planet in general.

6.2 Examining the cascading effects on other species, habitats, and even human communities.

Inspecting the flowing impacts of natural changes on different species, living spaces, and, surprisingly, human networks divulges a perplexing exchange of biological elements that rises above individual species and environments. The complicated snare of life on Earth is portrayed by interconnected connections where the prosperity of one animal categories frequently relies upon the strength of others and the solidness of their common territories.

As natural changes, driven by human exercises, overflow through biological systems, the repercussions reach out a long ways past the quick effect on a solitary animal varieties. This assessment dives into the flowing impacts on biodiversity, biological systems, and the more extensive ramifications for human networks, featuring the requirement for a comprehensive way to deal with ecological stewardship.

1. **Biodiversity and Interconnectedness:**
   Biodiversity is the bedrock of sound environments, addressing the assortment of life structures on The planet. The flowing impacts of ecological changes on different species are complicatedly attached to the interconnectedness of biodiversity. Every species, whether plant, creature, or microorganism, adds to the working of biological systems through complex connections, like predation, contest, and mutualism.

2. **Trophic Connections and Food Networks:**
   One of the essential ways natural changes influence different species is through adjustments in trophic connections and food networks. Trophic levels address positions in the well established pecking order, with each level ward on the one underneath it for energy move. As natural variables shift, affecting the overflow or conveyance of specific species, it disturbs the sensitive equilibrium of food networks, prompting flowing impacts all through the environment.

3. **Hierarchical and Base Up Impacts:**
   Flowing impacts can appear as hierarchical or base up impacts inside biological systems. Hierarchical impacts happen when changes at the most noteworthy trophic levels, like the downfall of hunters, impact the wealth of species at lower trophic levels. On the other hand, base up impacts

include changes in essential makers, like plants, influencing the overflow and elements of herbivores and ensuing trophic levels.

4. **Cornerstone Species and Biological system Specialists:**
Certain species, named cornerstone species and biological system engineers, excessively affect environments. The misfortune or adjustment of these species can set off flowing impacts all through whole biological systems. Cornerstone species apply impact past their mathematical overflow, while biological system engineers, through environment change, make conditions that benefit different species. Changes to these vital participants can have broad results.

5. **Herbivore-Plant Cooperations:**
The communications among herbivores and plants represent the flowing impacts that can happen inside biological systems. Changes in herbivore populaces, whether because of environment shifts, living space misfortune, or other natural elements, can prompt changes in vegetation elements. Overgrazing or the downfall of herbivores can bring about uncontrolled plant development, changing the creation of plant networks and affecting species subject to explicit vegetation types.

6. **Fertilization Elements and Plant Proliferation:**
Fertilization, an imperative biological system administration given by species like honey bees, butterflies, and birds, outlines the flowing impacts on plant generation. Ecological changes, including the utilization of pesticides, territory misfortune, and environment vacillations, influence pollinator populaces. The downfall of pollinators upsets the conceptive progress of blooming plants, influencing the overflow and variety of plant species inside biological systems.

7. **Flowing Consequences for Freshwater Environments:**
Freshwater environments, including streams and lakes, are especially vulnerable to flowing impacts. Changes in water quality, temperature, and stream influence oceanic species, including fish, creatures of land and water, and spineless creatures. These progressions resound through the food web, influencing hunter prey connections, supplement cycling, and the general wellbeing of freshwater environments.

8. **Maritime Fountains and Marine Biodiversity:**
Marine biological systems, enveloping huge maritime conditions, are additionally liable to flowing impacts. Overfishing, environmental change, and contamination can upset marine food networks, prompting decreases in fish populaces, changes in the wealth of marine hunters, and changes in the conveyance of planktonic species. These flowing impacts present dangers to marine biodiversity and the vocations of networks subject to fisheries.

9. **Environment Misfortune and Discontinuity:**
   Environment misfortune and discontinuity are significant drivers of flowing consequences for species and biological systems. As human exercises change scenes through deforestation, urbanization, and farming extension, environments become divided and detached. This discontinuity disturbs movement designs, limits hereditary trade among populaces, and expands the weakness of species to nearby terminations.

10. **Obtrusive Species and Biological Interruption:**
    The presentation of obtrusive species is a huge impetus for flowing impacts inside biological systems. Obtrusive species can outcompete local widely varied vegetation, present new sicknesses, and adjust territory structures. These disturbances can prompt decreases in local species, changes in biological system design, and difficulties for the networks subject to the administrations given by these environments.

11. **Flowing Impacts on Human People group:**
    The flowing impacts of natural changes reach out past biological domains, affecting human networks in different ways. Changes in biodiversity and environments can straightforwardly influence human prosperity, occupations, and financial frameworks. The deficiency of environment administrations, like clean water, prolific soil, and fertilization, presents direct dangers to agribusiness, food security, and general wellbeing.

12. **Farming and Food Security:**
    Farming frameworks are unpredictably associated with biodiversity and environment administrations. Changes in pollinator populaces, soil wellbeing, and water accessibility straightforwardly influence crop yields and horticultural efficiency. The deficiency of biodiversity can prompt the debasement of horticultural scenes, diminishing the strength of cultivating frameworks to vermin, illnesses, and ecological burdens.

13. **Environmental Change and Weakness:**
    Environmental change, driven by human exercises, is a significant driver of flowing impacts on the two biological systems and human networks. Increasing temperatures, adjusted precipitation examples, and outrageous climate occasions influence the appropriation and wealth of species, disturb rural practices, and add to the heightening of catastrophic events. Weak people group, especially those in low-lying waterfront regions or bone-dry locales, face expanded dangers and difficulties.

14. **Social and Native Effects:**
    Native people group, frequently profoundly associated with their indigenous habitats, experience significant effects from flowing natural changes. The deficiency of conventional scenes, changes in the accessibility of socially critical species, and disturbances to environmental cycles influence the social practices, personality, and prosperity of native populaces.

Protecting biodiversity is vital to supporting the social extravagance and variety of these networks.

15. **Financial Outcomes and Worldwide Equity:**
Flowing impacts on biodiversity and biological systems have financial results that frequently compound existing disparities. Weak people group, particularly in agricultural nations, may endure the worst part of ecological changes, confronting difficulties like food uncertainty, loss of occupations, and expanded weakness to environment related fiascos. Tending to these worldwide equity issues requires an aggregate obligation to reasonable turn of events and natural stewardship.

16. **Protection Methodologies and Versatile Administration:**
Moderating the flowing impacts of ecological changes requires thorough protection procedures and versatile administration draws near. Protection endeavors ought to zero in on saving basic living spaces, reestablishing debased biological systems, and executing feasible asset the executives rehearses. Versatile administration includes nonstop checking and change of protection procedures in view of developing ecological circumstances.

17. **Worldwide Participation and Strategy:**
Given the worldwide idea of flowing ecological impacts, global collaboration is principal. Multilateral arrangements, like the Show on Natural Variety (CBD) and the Paris Settlement on environmental change, give systems to cooperative activity. Policymakers assume a critical part in carrying out guidelines that advance economical practices, safeguard biodiversity, and address the underlying drivers of natural debasement.

18. **Instruction and Public Mindfulness:**

Instruction and public mindfulness crusades are fundamental parts of tending to the flowing impacts of ecological changes. Encouraging a comprehension of the interconnectedness between human exercises, biodiversity, and biological systems enables people and networks to pursue informed decisions.

Ecological proficiency advances economical practices and energizes aggregate activity towards a more agreeable conjunction with the normal world.All in all, analyzing the flowing impacts of ecological changes on different species, environments, and human networks highlights the multifaceted snare of interdependencies that describes our planet.

The all encompassing way to deal with natural stewardship requires perceiving the interconnectedness of biological frameworks and human social orders. Safeguarding biodiversity, reestablishing environments, and advancing reasonable practices are moral goals as well as fundamental stages towards guaranteeing the versatility and prosperity of the whole biosphere. The aggregate liability to address flowing impacts stretches out across nearby, public

6.3 Illustrating the concept of biodiversity as a stabilizing force.

Outlining the idea of biodiversity as a settling force uncovers the significant job that the assortment of life on Earth plays in keeping up with the equilibrium and strength of environments. Biodiversity incorporates the lavishness of species, hereditary variety inside species, and the range of environments that aggregately structure the complicated embroidery of life. This conversation dives into the diverse manners by which biodiversity goes about as a balancing out force, impacting biological capabilities, versatility to ecological changes, and the general strength of the planet.

****1. Environment Works and Administrations:**

One of the major manners by which biodiversity fills in as a balancing out force is through its impact on biological system works and administrations. Biological systems, made out of different species cooperating in complex ways, give a large number of administrations fundamental for life on The planet. Biodiversity adds to cycles like fertilization, water cleaning, supplement cycling, and environment guideline. These capabilities, all in all known as biological system administrations, support the steadiness of environments and their ability to help life.

2. Hereditary Variety and Variation:

Inside species, hereditary variety goes about as a settling force by upgrading versatility and strength. Hereditary variety addresses the range of hereditary characteristics inside a populace, permitting species to answer changing natural circumstances. Despite difficulties like illnesses, vermin, or changes in environment, hereditarily assorted populaces are better prepared to develop and adjust, guaranteeing the diligence of species after some time.

3. Trophic Connections and Food Networks:

Biodiversity assumes a significant part in molding trophic connections and food networks inside biological systems. Trophic connections address the exchange of energy through various levels of the pecking order, from makers to customers and decomposers. A different cluster of animal types guarantees that energy streams proficiently through these trophic levels, keeping up with the equilibrium of hunter prey connections and forestalling the overpopulation of specific species, which could disturb environment solidness.

4. Strength to Natural Changes:

Biodiversity adds to the strength of biological systems even with natural changes. Different environments are better ready to endure and recuperate from aggravations, whether they be normal occasions like rapidly spreading fires or human-prompted tensions like contamination. The range of species inside an environment gives a cushion against the effects of unsettling influences, taking into consideration the framework to quickly return and keep up with its usefulness.

5. Cornerstone Species and Environment Designers:

Certain species, named cornerstone species and environment engineers, apply lopsided impacts on the construction and capability of biological systems. Cornerstone species assume basic parts in keeping up with biodiversity, and their evacuation can prompt flowing impacts all through the biological system. Biological system engineers, through exercises like living space alteration, make conditions that benefit different species. These central participants go about as balancing out powers, impacting the elements of whole environments.

6. Environment Guideline and Carbon Sequestration:

Biodiversity contributes essentially to environment guideline, with woodlands, wetlands, and different biological systems assuming a critical part in carbon sequestration. Trees, for instance, retain carbon dioxide during photosynthesis and store carbon in their biomass.

Various biological systems with an assortment of plant animal varieties can sequester more carbon and assist with relieving the effects of environmental change. The deficiency of biodiversity lessens the limit of environments to go about as successful carbon sinks.

7. Soil Richness and Supplement Cycling:

In earthly biological systems, biodiversity impacts soil fruitfulness and supplement cycling. Different plant species have extraordinary root designs and supplement prerequisites, upgrading the productivity of supplement cycling in the dirt. Microorganisms, parasites, and decomposers make light of fundamental jobs in breaking natural matter and reusing supplements. The variety of these dirt life forms adds to the strength and richness of environments.

8. Infection Guideline:

Biodiversity goes about as a characteristic controller of sicknesses inside biological systems. The variety of species can restrict the spread of sicknesses by going about as cradles, forestalling the fast transmission of microbes. Certain species, known as "weakening hosts," can lessen the pervasiveness of sicknesses by diminishing the wealth of illness conveying organic entities. This administrative job features the significance of biodiversity in keeping up with the strength of both normal and rural frameworks.

9. Social and Stylish Qualities:

Biodiversity holds social and stylish qualities that add to the prosperity of human social orders. Native societies frequently have profound associations with their indigenous habitats, taking into account biodiversity as basic to their personalities and practices. Furthermore, the stylish worth of different scenes, going from rich rainforests to dynamic coral reefs, upgrades human encounters and cultivates a feeling of miracle and appreciation for the normal world.

10. Ecotourism and Monetary Advantages:

The idea of biodiversity as a balancing out force stretches out to financial advantages through exercises like ecotourism. Various biological systems, wealthy in biodiversity, draw in travelers keen on encountering special vegetation. The monetary worth got from ecotourism gives a motivator to the protection and practical administration of biodiverse regions, stressing the interconnectedness between biodiversity, financial flourishing, and human prosperity.

11. Horticulture and Food Security:

Biodiversity is principal to farming and worldwide food security. Crop variety, including various assortments of staple yields, guarantees versatility to nuisances, infections, and changing ecological circumstances. Hereditary variety in horticultural yields is pivotal for rearing new assortments that can adjust to developing difficulties. Also, the variety of pollinators adds to the effective multiplication of numerous food crops.

12. Drug Assets and Medication:

Biodiversity fills in as a rich wellspring of drug assets, with many plants, creatures, and microorganisms giving mixtures utilized in medication. The variety of living things offers an immense supply of likely restorative specialists. The deficiency of biodiversity reduces this drug potential as well as limits our capacity to find new medicines for different ailments.

13. Worldwide Interconnectedness:

The settling power of biodiversity isn't restricted to individual environments yet reaches out to the worldwide interconnectedness of Earth's frameworks. Changes in a single region of the planet can have expansive impacts on biodiversity and environments somewhere else. For instance, deforestation in tropical districts can impact environment designs worldwide, underscoring the requirement for composed global endeavors to protect biodiversity and keep up with the soundness of the whole planet.

14. Preservation Systems and Safeguarded Regions:

Protection systems assume a critical part in safeguarding biodiversity as a balancing out force. Laying out and successfully overseeing safeguarded regions, for example, public parks and natural life saves, give shelters to assorted species and environments. Preservation endeavors additionally include practical asset the executives, living space rebuilding, and tending to the main drivers of biodiversity misfortune, including deforestation and over-double-dealing.

15. Instruction and Mindfulness:

The idea of biodiversity as a settling force is complicatedly attached to the comprehension and enthusiasm for the regular world. Training and mindfulness crusades assume a significant part in encouraging a more profound appreciation for biodiversity and its significance for the solidness of biological systems. Ecological instruction engages people to pursue informed decisions that add to the protection and reasonable utilization of biodiversity.

All in all, outlining the idea of biodiversity as a balancing out force highlights the multifaceted and imperative job that different living things play in keeping up with the harmony of environments. From the guideline of natural capabilities to the arrangement of fundamental administrations, biodiversity fills in as a key part for the security and versatility of the planet. Perceiving and esteeming the different embroidery of life isn't just a biological objective yet in addition fundamental for guaranteeing the prosperity of human social orders and the supportability of the World's environments. As mankind wrestles with ecological difficulties, the safeguarding of biodiversity remains as a foundation for building an amicable and strong future for a long time into the future.

CHAPTER 7

Endangered Symphony

The "Imperiled Ensemble" repeats a piercing story of the speeding up loss of biodiversity, an emergency that compromises the multifaceted orchestra of life on The planet. This ensemble, made out of heap species communicating in agreeable environments, is confronting remarkable difficulties driven by human exercises. This talk dives into the causes, outcomes, and possible answers for the "Imperiled Ensemble," investigating the natural, financial, and moral components of biodiversity misfortune.

1. **The Suggestion of Biodiversity:**
   The suggestion of biodiversity makes way for life on The planet, incorporating the amazing assortment of creatures, environments, and hereditary variety. This orchestra isn't just a demonstration of the magnificence of nature yet a practical troupe where every species assumes a novel part, adding to the steadiness and versatility of biological systems. From the minute universe of microbes to the glory of dominant hunters, biodiversity organizes an ensemble that has developed more than great many years.

2. **The Crescendo of Eradication:**
   Notwithstanding, the crescendo of annihilation takes steps to upset this mind boggling ensemble. Human exercises, going from territory obliteration and contamination to environmental change and over-double-dealing, have moved numerous species towards the cliff of termination. The ongoing pace of species misfortune is disturbing, outperforming normal foundation elimination rates by an extent that repeats the mass termination occasions of Earth's topographical history.

3. **Reasons for the Dissonant Notes:**
   The dissonant notes in the "Imperiled Orchestra" track down their beginnings in anthropogenic exercises. Natural surroundings annihilation,

energized by deforestation, urbanization, and modern development, leaves species without reasonable homes. Contamination, from synthetics to plastics, taints environments and postures direct dangers to incalculable creatures. Environmental change, an outcome of extreme ozone harming substance discharges, modifies temperature and precipitation designs, disturbing the sensitive equilibrium of biological systems.

4. **The Anthropocene Period:**

We wind up in the Anthropocene time, described by human predominance and effect on Earth's frameworks. The results of our activities resound through the "Imperiled Orchestra," with eliminations happening at rates that mark this age as a basic crossroads in the planet's set of experiences. The Anthropocene requests reflection on our job as stewards of biodiversity and the moral ramifications of our effect on the worldwide ensemble of life.

5. **Deficiency of Cornerstone Players:**

Inside the "Imperiled Ensemble," certain species go about as cornerstone players, applying lopsided impact on their environments. The deficiency of these cornerstones can prompt flowing impacts, disturbing the amicability of whole environments. Hunters, like wolves or sharks, keep up with balance by controlling prey populaces. The vanishing of these essential players slants the environmental scales, intensifying the gamble of uncontrolled populace blasts and the expected breakdown of whole biological systems.

6. **Reverberations of Eradication Across Trophic Levels:**

The reverberations of termination resonate across trophic levels, influencing the sensitive interchange inside food networks. As species vanish, the unpredictable dance of predation, contest, and mutualism flounders. The termination of pollinators, like honey bees and butterflies, risks the proliferation of various plant species, influencing biodiversity as well as compromising worldwide food security.

7. **Interruption of Relocation and Territories:**

Movement, a crucial part of many species' life cycles, faces disturbance in the "Jeopardized Orchestra." Anthropogenic exercises, including environment fracture and environmental change, obstruct conventional relocation courses. Birds, warm blooded creatures, and, surprisingly, marine species find their processes impeded, prompting diminished reproducing achievement, changed ways of behaving, and lessened hereditary variety.

8. **The Worldwide Exchange Ensemble:**

The worldwide exchange of natural life, driven by interest for outlandish pets, customary prescriptions, and elaborate species, adds to the disharmony inside the "Jeopardized Orchestra." Impractical exchange rehearses, combined with unlawful dealing, drive various species to the edge of eradication. Endeavors to battle this issue include worldwide collaboration, stricter guidelines, and bringing issues to light about the moral results of untamed life exchange.

9. **Monetary Disagreements:**
The monetary disagreements coming from biodiversity misfortune stretch out a long ways past natural domains. Numerous people group depend straightforwardly on biodiversity for their occupations, whether through farming, fisheries, or ecotourism. The breakdown of fisheries, for instance, imperils marine biodiversity as well as risks the prosperity of millions who rely upon fisheries for food and work.

10. **Therapeutic Quieting:**
The "Jeopardized Ensemble" remembers a part for the quieting of restorative assets. Numerous drugs are gotten from plants, creatures, and microorganisms. As species vanish, possible solutions for infections might evaporate before they are even found. The deficiency of biodiversity subsequently influences environments as well as hampers mankind's capability to open the mysteries of nature for restorative purposes.

11. **Moral Discord:**
Biodiversity misfortune brings up moral issues about humankind's liability to safeguard the "Imperiled Orchestra." The termination of species addresses the deletion of interesting types of life that have developed over centuries. The moral discord lies in the acknowledgment that our activities, driven by momentary additions, are prompting the irreversible loss of biodiversity and the likely upright obligation regarding the outcomes on people in the future.

12. **Preservation Rhythm:**
To address the discord inside the "Jeopardized Orchestra," preservation endeavors should frame an amicable rhythm. Preservation systems include the foundation of safeguarded regions, practical asset the executives, environment reclamation, and local area commitment. These endeavors point not exclusively to save individual species yet to defend the respectability and usefulness of whole biological systems.

13. **Ensemble of Reclamation:**
The "Ensemble of Reclamation" is a contrast to the discord of biodiversity misfortune. Reclamation drives, for example, reforestation activities and living space restoration, add to the recuperation of environments. By once again introducing cornerstone species, revamping debased natural surroundings, and tending to the underlying drivers of ecological corruption, the orchestra of reclamation tries to fix a portion of the harm caused upon Earth's biodiversity.

14. **Congruity Through Economical Practices:**
Congruity inside the "Imperiled Ensemble" can be accomplished through

supportable practices that focus on the drawn out prosperity of biological systems. Supportable farming, capable fishing rehearses, and moral the travel industry add to a more agreeable connection among mankind and nature. These practices plan to offset human necessities with the basic to safeguard biodiversity for people in the future.

15. **Schooling as a Blending Power:**
Instruction arises as a blending force inside the "Jeopardized Ensemble." Ecological training cultivates mindfulness, understanding, and a feeling of obligation towards biodiversity. By imparting an affection for nature, moral contemplations, and an appreciation for the interconnectedness of life, training turns into a strong instrument in coordinating a more agreeable connection among mankind and the normal world.

16. **Worldwide Agreement:**
The idea of worldwide agreement inside the "Jeopardized Orchestra" highlights the requirement for global collaboration. Biodiversity knows no boundaries, and its conservation requires an aggregate responsibility from countries, networks, and people. Worldwide arrangements, like the Show on Organic Variety (CBD), give systems to cooperative activity, underscoring the common obligation of all countries in shielding Earth's biodiversity.

17. **The Quiet Tribute to People in the future:**
The "Jeopardized Orchestra" conveys a quiet tribute to people in the future. The choices we make today will resonate through time, forming the world that our relatives acquire. The disharmony of biodiversity misfortune provokes us to create an amicable inheritance — one where the orchestra of life keeps on prospering, giving motivation, miracle, and food for ages yet unborn.

18. **The Criticalness of Now:**

In the last development of the "Imperiled Orchestra," the desperation of now reverberates. There's no time to waste as species waver near the precarious edge of termination. The open door to switch biodiversity misfortune is shutting quickly. The orchestra of life calls for prompt and purposeful activity to address the main drivers, execute preservation methodologies, and cultivate an amicable conjunction among humankind and the normal world.

All in all, the "Jeopardized Ensemble" is a dismal yet confident piece that urges mankind to reexamine its relationship with the normal world. The harsh notes of biodiversity misfortune request a purposeful work to reestablish concordance inside environments.

The ensemble of life, with its bunch species and many-sided connections, welcomes us to become stewards of the Earth, guaranteeing that the music of biodiversity keeps on resounding for a long time into the future. As we defy the difficulties of the Anthropocene, the open door exists to form another development — one that fits human exercises with the rhythms of the planet, making a tradition of equilibrium, strength, and getting through biodiversity.

7.1 Portraying the interconnectedness of species as a symphony.

Depicting the interconnectedness of species as an ensemble divulges an entrancing story of life on The planet, where the horde living beings, environments, and biological cycles fit in a complicated coordination. This figurative ensemble highlights the reliance of species, representing how each note, every species, adds to the organization of a fantastic biological show-stopper. This investigation digs into the different developments of this ensemble, stressing the jobs of biodiversity, trophic connections, mutualisms, and the complicated snare of life that ties the planet's assorted occupants into a musical solidarity.

1. **The Suggestion of Biodiversity:**
   The suggestion of this orchestra is played by biodiversity, the huge swath of life shapes that populate the Earth. Biodiversity is the director organizing the many-sided songs of biological systems, from the infinitesimal to the plainly visible.
   The orchestra starts with the variety of qualities, species, and environments, each contributing an interesting tone to the general structure. Biodiversity guarantees the strength and versatility of life, making a rich embroidery that includes a stunning assortment of structures, capabilities, and collaborations.

2. **Trophic Connections as Consonant Movements:**
   Trophic connections structure the consonant movements inside the ensemble of interconnected species. The idea of trophic levels addresses the various situations in the pecking order, with makers, customers, and decomposers each assuming an unmistakable part. This unique cooperation lays out a melodic continuum, where each trophic level is a note adding to the general concordance of environments. The herbivores touch like a delicate song, the hunters reverberate with a strong crescendo, and the decomposers make an unobtrusive hint, finishing the amicable pattern of life.

3. **Hunters and Prey in Sweet Pursuits:**
   Inside the ensemble, hunters and prey take part in sweet pursuits that shape the elements of environments. The hunter prey collaborations make a fragile dance, a musical back and forth movement that keeps up with the equilibrium of populaces. Hunters, as talented performers, keep any one animal groups from ruling the stage, guaranteeing a different and dynamic presentation. The quest for prey and the avoidance of hunters

make a unique development, a demonstration of the finely tuned connections that portray the interconnectedness of species.

4. **Mutualisms as Two part harmony Organizations:**
Mutualisms, the harmonious organizations between various species, arise as two part harmony associations inside the ensemble. These cooperative connections, where the two species benefit, reverberation an agreeable two part harmony where each accomplice upgrades the capacities of the other. Models proliferate, from fertilization organizations among blossoms and pollinators to the commonly useful connections between specific plants and parasites. These two part harmonies highlight the possibility that in the ensemble of life, collaboration is just about as necessary as contest.

5. **The Concordance of Biological system Administrations:**
Biological system administrations reverberate all through the ensemble, addressing the unmistakable and immaterial advantages that environments give to mankind. Clean air, new water, fertilization, environment guideline, and supplement cycling are the harmonies that support life on The planet.
The ensemble of environment administrations is a complex creation that highlights the interconnectedness of species and biological systems with human prosperity. Disturbances to this concordance, like biodiversity misfortune, resonate through the whole ensemble, influencing the personal satisfaction for all species.

6. **The Mood of Transformation and Advancement:**
Variation and development set the mood of the ensemble, exhibiting the capacity of species to change and change after some time. The orchestra of variation is a powerful interaction where animal groups answer natural changes, guaranteeing natural selection. Developmental rhythms make new varieties, adding intricacy and variety to the orchestra. The interconnectedness of species is apparent in the common history of life, where the songs of antiquated predecessors resound in the hereditary sytheses of their relatives.

7. **Microbial Crescendos:**
Microbial living things contribute crescendos to the ensemble, frequently disregarded yet principal to the organization of environments. Microorganisms assume parts in supplement cycling, soil wellbeing, and the absorption cycles of different living beings. These minute crescendos intensify the intricacy of the ensemble, helping us that the interconnectedness to remember species traverses the whole range of life, from the littlest microorganisms to the biggest well evolved creatures.

8. **The Melody of Relocation:**
Relocation adds an ensemble to the orchestra, where species get across

scenes and seas, adding to the unique developments of biological systems. Birds cross landmasses, whales explore tremendous seas, and ungulates leave on awe-inspiring movements.This melody of relocation upgrades hereditary variety, works with fertilization, and shapes the appropriation of species. The interconnectedness of environments becomes clear as transient species interface far off living spaces, impacting the creation and capability of biological systems across their reaches. The ensemble of movement is a demonstration of the consistent coordination of species, displaying their capacity to rise above geological limits in quest for endurance, propagation, and asset accessibility.

9. **The Agreement of Cornerstone Species:**
Cornerstone species assume a part likened to soloists inside the orchestra, applying a lopsided effect on the design and capability of environments. Their effect reverberates a long ways past their mathematical overflow. Whether it's the presence of wolves keeping up with the equilibrium of prey populaces or the action of beavers forming sea-going territories, cornerstone species contribute exceptional songs that characterize the personality of whole environments. The deficiency of these central members can prompt environmental cacophony, highlighting the fragile idea of interconnected species.

10. **Disharmony in the Anthropocene:**
The orchestra experiences discord in the Anthropocene period, an age set apart by human impact in the world. Anthropogenic exercises, like deforestation, contamination, and environmental change, present harsh notes that compromise the concordance of the interconnected species. The Anthropocene development in the orchestra mirrors the criticalness of addressing human-prompted disturbances and tracking down ways of reestablishing balance inside the multifaceted snare of life.

11. **The Moral Abstain:**
A moral abstain pervades the orchestra, encouraging humankind to recognize its job as both author and director. The interconnectedness of species requests moral contemplations in the utilization of assets, preservation endeavors, and feasible practices. The moral hold back welcomes reflection on the obligation of people to go about as stewards of the Earth, guaranteeing the proceeded with presence of the orchestra for people in the future.

12. **The Quiet Creation of Eradication:**
Inside the ensemble, the quiet piece of eradication creates a solemn shaded area. Species vanish, their songs hushed until the end of time. The interconnectedness of species turns out to be horrendously obvious as the deficiency of one animal varieties can set off a flowing impact, upsetting the whole piece. The quiet notes of termination act as a strong wake up

call of the irreversible outcomes of human exercises on the mind boggling orchestra of life.

13. **The Guide's Cudgel of Protection:**
Preservation endeavors employ the director's twirly doo inside the orchestra, directing mediations to safeguard and reestablish biodiversity. Safeguarded regions, living space reclamation, and maintainable asset the executives become the instruments to protect the harmonies of biological systems. The guide's twirly doo of protection underlines the requirement for aggregate activity, worldwide cooperation, and a common obligation to shielding the interconnectedness of species.

14. **Biodiversity as a Worldwide Ensemble:**
The depiction of the interconnectedness of species stretches out to a worldwide ensemble where biological systems, environments, and species are interlinked across landmasses. The Amazon rainforest influences atmospheric conditions in far off districts, polar ice dissolve impacts ocean levels around the world, and transitory species associate environments across borders. The worldwide orchestra highlights the truth that the prosperity of any species, including people, is unpredictably attached to the wellbeing and working of the whole planet.

15. **Environmental Change as a Crescendo:**
Environmental change arises as a strong crescendo inside the orchestra, intensifying the difficulties looked by interconnected species. Climbing temperatures, changed precipitation examples, and outrageous climate occasions make a conflicting setting that strains the versatility of biological systems. The orchestra of variation battles to stay up with the fast changes, featuring the requirement for worldwide participation to moderate environmental change and lighten its effects on biodiversity.

16. **The Crescendo of Joint effort:**
Joint effort turns into a crescendo inside the ensemble, underscoring the interconnectedness of species across different biological systems and human social orders. Worldwide arrangements, like the Show on Natural Variety, become the score for worldwide collaboration, stressing the common obligation of countries to safeguard biodiversity. The crescendo of cooperation highlights the acknowledgment that the orchestra of life is an aggregate undertaking that rises above borders and requires brought together endeavors.

17. **The Tune of Trust and Rebuilding:**
In the midst of the difficulties and disharmony, the orchestra resounds with the song of trust and reclamation. Protection triumphs, reforestation ventures, and local area drove drives make harmonies that show the versatility of interconnected species. The song of trust energizes people,

networks, and countries to take part in the organization of a more amicable future for the orchestra of life effectively.

18. **The Reprise of Stewardship:**

As the orchestra arrives at its last notes, the reprise of stewardship arises. The interconnectedness of species requires an aggregate obligation to mindful and feasible practices. Every individual turns into a steward, adding to the safeguarding of biodiversity through day to day decisions, protection mindfulness, and a profound appreciation for the agreeable ensemble that characterizes life on The planet.

All in all, depicting the interconnectedness of species as an ensemble is a similitude that exemplifies the excellence, intricacy, and delicacy of life on The planet. The ensemble highlights the requirement for concordance, preservation, and moral contemplations in the communications among species and their surroundings. The interconnectedness of species isn't simply a logical idea; it is a no nonsense ensemble that welcomes us to tune in, appreciate, and effectively take part in the continuous structure of life on our planet.

7.2 Emphasizing the unique role each species plays in maintaining ecological harmony.

Underlining the one of a kind job every animal varieties plays in keeping up with environmental concordance reveals the unpredictable dance of life on The planet, where each living being adds to the orchestra of biological systems. This investigation digs into the meaning of biodiversity, the practical jobs of species inside environments, and the fragile equilibrium that supports the many-sided trap of life. It features the bunch manners by which every species, from the littlest microorganisms to the biggest dominant hunters, has an unmistakable and indispensable impact in keeping up with biological concordance.

1. **Biodiversity as the Ensemble of Life:**
   Biodiversity fills in as the ensemble of life, enveloping the range of species, qualities, and environments that coincide on The planet. This lavishness is definitely not an irregular grouping; rather, it is a finely tuned sythesis where every species contributes a remarkable note. Biodiversity is the entirety of this multitude of notes, making an agreeable orchestra that characterizes the wellbeing and strength of biological systems. Underlining the exceptional job of every species inside this ensemble is essential for understanding and safeguarding the sensitive equilibrium of biological concordance.

2. **Cornerstone Species as Guides:**
   Inside the symphony of biodiversity, certain species arise as directors — cornerstone species that apply a lopsided effect on the construction and

capability of biological systems. These species, whether hunters, pollinators, or biological system engineers, assume crucial parts in keeping up with environmental amicability. Wolves, for instance, control prey populaces, forestalling overgrazing and advancing plant variety. Honey bees, as pollinators, guarantee the propagation of various plant species. The arrangement of these cornerstone species is fundamental for the general wellbeing and security of biological systems.

3. **Trophic Fountains and Consonant Reverberation:**
   Trophic fountains epitomize the symphonious reverberation inside biological systems, outlining how changes in a single animal types can resonate through whole food networks. The presence or nonattendance of top hunters can flow down trophic levels, affecting the wealth of species and forming the arrangement of networks. The consonant reverberation of trophic fountains underlines that every species, whether at the top or lower part of the natural pecking order, adds to the general equilibrium and design of environments.

4. **Subject matter experts and Generalists as Instrumentalists:**
   Species can be compared to instrumentalists inside the natural ensemble, with trained professionals and generalists assuming particular parts. Expert species, finely tuned to explicit environments or food sources, contribute one of a kind songs to the ensemble. Generalists, versatile and adaptable, give a cadenced suggestion, guaranteeing the adaptability and flexibility of environments. Underscoring the jobs of the two subject matter experts and generalists features the variety of methodologies that species utilize to flourish in their separate specialties.

5. **Environment Designers as Engineers:**
   Biological system engineers, like beavers, corals, and insects, capability as planners inside the environmental scene. These species adjust environments, making structures that impact the physical and natural attributes of biological systems. Beavers, through dam-building, shape oceanic conditions, while corals develop complex reef biological systems. The building commitments of environment engineers highlight their remarkable job in making and keeping up with natural surroundings that help a huge number of different species.

6. **The Amicability of Mutualisms:**
   Mutualistic connections between species make harmonies inside the natural ensemble. Models flourish, from the fertilization associations among blossoms and their pollinators to the commonly gainful connections between specific plants and organisms. These harmonies underscore the relationship of species, where participation and shared help upgrade the wellness and endurance of the members. Stressing the one of a kind jobs

in mutualistic communications highlights the complicated associations that add to biological congruity.

7. **Microbial Maestros in Soil:**
Microorganisms, frequently concealed however massively powerful, go about as maestros in the dirt symphony. Microorganisms, parasites, and different organisms assume fundamental parts in supplement cycling, decay, and soil wellbeing.
The microbial symphony in soil highlights the primary job these living beings play in supporting plant development, keeping up with soil structure, and adding to the general richness of environments. Each microbial species plays an extraordinary part in organizing these cycles, underlining their singular commitments to environmental concordance.

8. **Specialty Specialization and Natural Agreement:**
Specialty specialization, where species adjust to explicit jobs and environments, is a vital component in keeping up with natural congruity. Every species possesses a one of a kind natural specialty, characterized by its communications with different species and its part in environment processes. The variety of specialties considers the productive utilization of assets and the evasion of direct rivalry, adding to the general security and versatility of environments. Stressing the significance of specialty specialization features the complicated embroidery woven by various species in their environmental jobs.

9. **Hereditary Variety as Melodic Variety:**
Hereditary variety inside species goes about as melodic variety inside the natural orchestra. The unrefined substance permits populaces to adjust to changing ecological circumstances. The exceptional hereditary cosmetics of people inside an animal groups adds to the general flexibility and developmental capability of that species. Underlining the significance of hereditary variety highlights the job it plays in guaranteeing the versatile limit of species, especially even with natural changes.

10. **Social Commitments to Agreement:**
Ways of behaving displayed by various species add to the social elements of biological systems, adding subtleties to the environmental orchestra. For instance, seed dispersal by creatures, hunter prey associations, and mating ceremonies all address conduct angles that impact the design and capability of biological systems. Underscoring the social commitments of species features the complicated manners by which their activities shape the biological stories and add to the general agreement of environments.

11. **The Musical Dance of Transitory Species:**
Transient species participate in a musical dance, getting across scenes and interfacing different biological systems. Birds, well evolved creatures, and, surprisingly, marine species embrace epic excursions, adding to

the natural network of territories. The developments of transitory species impact supplement cycling, seed dispersal, and populace elements, making harmonies that resound across topographical limits. Stressing the job of transient species highlights their significance in keeping up with biological congruity on a worldwide scale.

12. **Biological system Administrations as Melodic Contributions:**
Biological system benefits, the advantages that environments give to mankind, should be visible as melodic contributions inside the natural orchestra. Clean air, water refinement, fertilization of yields, and environment guideline are administrations given by biological systems. Every species, whether straightforwardly or in a roundabout way, adds to these melodic contributions that help human prosperity. Underlining the association among species and biological system administrations highlights the inherent worth of biodiversity to human social orders.

13. **Protection as the Guide's Mallet:**
Preservation endeavors go about as the director's cudgel in the environmental symphony, directing mediations to secure and reestablish biodiversity. Safeguarded regions, natural surroundings rebuilding, and practical asset the executives become fundamental devices to save the one of a kind jobs of animal categories inside environments. Preservation fills in as the directing power that guarantees the proceeded with presence of every species and their commitments to the general agreement of environmental frameworks.

14. **The Interconnectedness of Species as a Melodic Score:**
The interconnectedness of species can be seen as a melodic score, where each note addresses an animal categories assuming its one of a kind part in the environmental sythesis. The course of action of these notes makes songs, harmonies, and rhythms that characterize the biological ensemble. Understanding the interconnectedness of species as a melodic score considers an all encompassing enthusiasm for the mind boggling connections that support life on The planet.

15. **Human Obligation as Caretakers of Amicability:**
As caretakers of natural concordance, people bear a significant obligation to perceive, appreciate, and ration the extraordinary jobs of every species. Anthropogenic exercises, from environment annihilation to contamination, bring grating notes into the biological orchestra. Recognizing our job as stewards includes embracing economical works on, supporting protection drives, and encouraging a profound regard for the perplexing trap of life. Human obligation turns into the directing song that fits with the normal rhythms of biological systems.

16. **Schooling as a Thunderous Harmony:**
Schooling arises as a thunderous harmony inside the orchestra,

encouraging mindfulness and comprehension of the extraordinary jobs played by every species. Natural instruction imparts a feeling of obligation, sympathy, and appreciation for biodiversity.

By underlining the significance of each and every species as one, schooling turns into a strong instrument in developing a preservation disapproved of society that effectively takes part in the security of the normal world.

17. **Environmental Change as a Grating Note:**

Environmental change brings a grating note into the natural orchestra, testing the versatile limits of species and biological systems. Increasing temperatures, adjusted precipitation examples, and outrageous climate occasions upset the finely tuned connections that characterize environmental concordance. Relieving environmental change becomes basic to safeguard the extraordinary jobs of species and keep up with the general equilibrium of biological systems.

18. **A Call for Coordinated Activity:**

All in all, stressing the exceptional job every species plays in keeping up with biological congruity is a call for purposeful activity to protect the perplexing ensemble of life. From cornerstone species to minuscule life forms, each contributes a particular note to the environmental piece. Perceiving, esteeming, and saving these exceptional jobs is fundamental for guaranteeing the proceeded with presence of biodiversity and the strength of environments. An aggregate undertaking requires worldwide collaboration, moral contemplations, and a common obligation to be mindful caretakers of the natural ensemble for present and people in the future.

7.3 Discussing the consequences of losing certain "notes" in the symphony.

Examining the results of losing certain "notes" in the ensemble reveals a story of biological unevenness and the potential disentangling of complex associations inside environments. This investigation dives into the flowing impacts, disturbances in trophic elements, and the more extensive environmental outcomes that emerge when key species, likened to melodic notes, are lost. It underlines the delicacy of biological systems and highlights the earnest need to perceive, secure, and reestablish the fundamental parts of the regular orchestra.

1. **The Despairing of Elimination:**

The results of losing certain "notes" in the natural ensemble are maybe generally tangibly felt through the despairing of annihilation. At the point when an animal varieties is lost, its interesting song is quieted perpetually, upsetting the amicable piece that has developed over centuries.

Elimination isn't just the vanishing of a solitary animal types; it addresses the deletion of an unmistakable arrangement of connections, ways of behaving, and environmental capabilities that were once essential to the orchestra of life.

2. **Disturbances in Trophic Elements:**
   The deficiency of key species resounds through trophic levels, causing disturbances in trophic elements that can prompt biological disorder. Consider the situation where a top hunter, like an enormous flesh eater, is lost. Without the controlling impact of this hunter, herbivore populaces might flood, bringing about overgrazing and the exhaustion of plant networks. The shortfall of this "note" in the trophic orchestra makes a disharmony that fountains through the biological system, influencing both widely varied vegetation.

3. **Flowing Consequences for Biological system Construction:**
   Flowing impacts unfurl when certain "notes" are lost, reshaping the actual design of biological systems. The vanishing of a cornerstone animal types, like a beaver or an ocean otter, can set off overflows that modify natural surroundings creation and accessibility. Beavers, for example, engineer wetland environments by building dams, affecting water stream, and making different living spaces. The deficiency of such instrumental "notes" can prompt worked on biological systems with lessened biodiversity, featuring the weakness of perplexing natural designs.

4. **Adjusted Populace Elements:**
   Certain species go about as administrative "notes" in keeping up with adjusted populace elements inside biological systems. Hunters, for example, hold prey populaces under wraps, forestalling overgrazing and guaranteeing the soundness of plant networks. The deficiency of these administrative "notes" can bring about uncontrolled populace blasts among specific species, prompting uneven characters that resound across trophic levels. This modified populace dynamic can have inescapable ramifications for the whole biological system, influencing both biodiversity and environment administrations.

5. **Influence on Mutualistic Connections:**
   The ensemble of mutualistic connections, where species work together for common advantage, can be seriously influenced by the deficiency of key members. Consider the interruption brought about by the downfall of pollinators, like honey bees and butterflies. These bugs are instrumental in the propagation of various blossoming plants. The deficiency of pollinators brings about a conflicting note, risking the multiplication of plants and influencing the whole local area that depends on these connections for endurance.

6. **Breakdown of Biological system Administrations:**
Biological system benefits, the significant commitments that environments make to human prosperity, face a critical future when certain "notes" are lost. Be it the fertilization of yields by bugs, the sanitization of water by wetland plants, or the guideline of environment by woods, these administrations depend on the different cluster of species inside biological systems. The breakdown of key species can think twice about conveyance of biological system administrations, undermining food security, water quality, and the soundness of worldwide environments.

7. **Weakness to Intrusive Species:**
The deficiency of certain "notes" in the biological orchestra can deliver environments more powerless against the attack of non-local species. Without a trace of key contenders, hunters, or sickness controllers, intrusive species might take advantage of empty environmental specialties, outcompeting or going after local species. This presents new and frequently troublesome "notes" into the orchestra, prompting adjusted local area elements, loss of biodiversity, and likely natural homogenization.

8. **Diminished Versatility to Natural Changes:**
Biological system versatility, the capacity to endure and recuperate from aggravations, is compromised when basic "notes" are lost. Flexibility frequently depends on the variety of species and their utilitarian jobs inside biological systems. The vanishing of specific species, particularly those with exceptional versatile characteristics or biological capabilities, debilitates the framework's ability to adapt to ecological changes. This diminished versatility intensifies the weakness of environments to stressors, for example, environmental change, living space corruption, and illness flare-ups.

9. **Influence on Social and Tasteful Qualities:**
Past biological results, the deficiency of certain "notes" in the ensemble has significant social and stylish ramifications. Numerous species hold social importance for human social orders, assuming parts in legends, customs, and profound convictions. Also, the stylish worth of biodiversity, saw in the dynamic shades of coral reefs, the complex examples of butterfly wings, or the eerie calls of jeopardized birds, is reduced when key species are lost. The social and stylish texture of human life is unpredictably woven with the biodiversity that encompasses us.

10. **Decline of Ecotourism Valuable open doors:**
Biodiversity misfortune can bring about the downfall of ecotourism potential open doors, influencing neighborhood economies and protection endeavors. Numerous districts rely upon the charm of different environments and appealling species to draw in vacationers. The vanishing of key species decreases the engaging quality of these objections, prompting

financial misfortunes for networks that depend on ecotourism for livelihoods. This monetary effect further highlights the interconnectedness between the prosperity of environments and human social orders.

11. **Moral Contemplations and Loss of Significant worth:**
The deficiency of certain "notes" in the ensemble raises significant moral contemplations. Every species has inherent worth, adding to the variety and extravagance of life on The planet. The elimination of an animal types addresses the irreversible loss of an exceptional type of life, and questions emerge about mankind's moral obligation to forestall such eradications. The acknowledgment of the inborn worth of every species accentuates the significance of protection endeavors and moral stewardship of biodiversity.

12. **The Combined Impact of Numerous Misfortunes:**
The results of losing certain "notes" in the orchestra are intensified by the total impact of numerous misfortunes. As species vanish, the interconnected trap of natural connections unwinds, making a cascading type of influence that intensifies the difficulties looked by environments. The combined loss of biodiversity prompts a scene where key capabilities are compromised, and biological systems battle to keep up with soundness and flexibility.

13. **The Cascading type of influence on Human Prosperity:**
The results of losing certain "notes" stretch out past environmental domains and straightforwardly affect human prosperity. The disturbance of environment administrations, decrease in food security, expanded weakness to cataclysmic events, and loss of social and sporting qualities on the whole make a cascading type of influence that influences the personal satisfaction for networks all over the planet. The interconnectedness among biological systems and human social orders features the basic of safeguarding the orchestra of biodiversity to support both.

14. **The Test of Natural Reclamation:**
Reestablishing the ensemble after certain "notes" have been lost presents a considerable test. Natural reclamation endeavors plan to once again introduce or restore species to restore useful biological systems. In any case, the intricacy of natural collaborations and the durable effects of species misfortune make rebuilding a fragile and unsure cycle. The test lies in reproducing the natural parts as well as in reestablishing the multifaceted connections that characterize biological agreement.

15. **Worldwide Ramifications and Planetary Wellbeing:**
The results of losing certain "notes" in the orchestra resound worldwide, adding to the more extensive issue of planetary wellbeing. Biodiversity misfortune, driven by human exercises, for example, environment obliteration, environmental change, and contamination, has broad ramifications

for the wellbeing of the whole planet. The interconnectedness of biological systems on a worldwide scale requires global collaboration and deliberate endeavors to address the underlying drivers of biodiversity decline and advance the reclamation of natural congruity.

16. **The Job of Protection as an Ensemble Guide:**
Protection arises as the ensemble guide entrusted with forestalling the deficiency of basic "notes" in the biological creation. Preservation endeavors include safeguarding natural surroundings, carrying out economical practices, and alleviating dangers like poaching and living space annihilation. The job of preservation stretches out past saving individual species; it envelops the shielding of whole environments and the mind boggling connections that support natural agreement.

17. **A Call for Worldwide Stewardship:**
The results of losing certain "notes" in the orchestra highlight the desperation of worldwide stewardship. Perceiving the interconnectedness of species and environments, countries and networks should team up to address the drivers of biodiversity misfortune. Peaceful accords, like the Show on Natural Variety, give structures to aggregate activity to secure and reestablish the orchestra of life. A call for worldwide stewardship stresses the common obligation of mankind in protecting the variety and versatility of the regular world.

18. **Trust in Reclamation and Preservation:**

In the midst of the conversation of results, there is trust in the force of reclamation and preservation. Fruitful preservation drives, living space reclamation undertakings, and local area drove endeavors show that it is feasible to switch a portion of the harm and reestablish lost "notes" in the orchestra. By recognizing the results of biodiversity misfortune, society can channel aggregate endeavors toward an amicable and manageable conjunction with the regular world, guaranteeing that the orchestra of life keeps on resounding for a long time into the future.

All in all, examining the results of losing certain "notes" in the orchestra gives a focal point through which to figure out the significant effects of biodiversity misfortune on biological systems, human social orders, and the strength of the planet. The allegorical orchestra of natural communications helps us to remember the fragile equilibrium kept up with by every species, and the obligation mankind bears as stewards of this perplexing creation. It is a source of inspiration to secure, reestablish, and praise the variety of life that improves the World's orchestra.

CHAPTER 8

Last Plea Dance

The "Last Supplication Dance" is a reminiscent representation that epitomizes the pressing and piercing sob for endurance produced by species near the very edge of elimination. This figurative dance addresses a last, frantic endeavor by jeopardized life forms to cause to notice their predicament, beseeching mankind to make a conclusive move to deflect their end. As we investigate the multi-layered components of the "Last Supplication Dance," we dig into the natural, moral, and close to home perspectives that highlight the basic requirement for protection and the conservation of biodiversity.

1. **The Dance of Environmental Distress:**
   The "Last Supplication Dance" unfurls as a powerful articulation of biological franticness. Species very nearly elimination take part in ways of behaving that might appear to be uncommon, lavish, or frantic — signs of a battle for endurance despite territory misfortune, environmental change, contamination, and other anthropogenic tensions. This figurative dance incorporates different versatile methodologies, from modified regenerative ways of behaving to escalated searching, as species endeavor to explore a changing and frequently unfriendly climate.

2. **Biodiversity's Quiet Cry:**
   The similitude of the "Last Request Dance" repeats biodiversity's quiet weep for consideration. As species vanish at a disturbing rate because of human exercises, the multifaceted snare of life is disentangling. This dance is a quiet yet strong correspondence, a supplication that resounds through biological systems, flagging the unwinding of the rich embroidery of biodiversity. The elimination emergency addresses a quiet cry that requests a reaction — an acknowledgment of the inborn worth of every species and the affirmation that their vanishing is a hopeless misfortune to the orchestra of life.

3. **Moral Appearance in the Movement:**
   The "Last Supplication Dance" prompts moral reflections on humankind's job as choreographer and observer. As stewards of the Earth, people hold a double job in molding the fate of species. decisions in asset use, preservation endeavors, and supportable practices decide if the dance proceeds or finishes up in sad quietness. Moral contemplations highlight the obligation to go about as humane choreographers, guaranteeing that the dance of life endures for a long time into the future.

4. **Human-Prompted Disharmony:**
   The disharmony presented by human exercises frames a dissonant setting to the "Last Supplication Dance." Territory obliteration, contamination, environmental change, and other anthropogenic elements upset the regular rhythms and songs of biological systems, constraining species into a frantic dance for endurance. This cacophony features the results of human-initiated natural lopsidedness and fills in as an unmistakable update that our activities have significant ramifications for the many-sided movement of life.

5. **The Orchestra of Protection:**
   Inside the setting of the "Last Supplication Dance," protection arises as the ensemble that endeavors to blend the dissonant notes presented by human exercises. Preservation endeavors, including territory insurance, rebuilding, and maintainable asset the executives, plan to reestablish the equilibrium and give a favorable climate to animal categories to flourish. The ensemble of preservation turns into a contradiction to the discord, offering trust and a pathway to relieve the effects of the anthropogenic dangers that move species into their last supplication for endurance.

6. **Close to home Reverberation of Misfortune:**
   The close to home reverberation of misfortune penetrates the "Last Request Dance." Seeing the decay of species and the reducing biodiversity inspires a significant feeling of misery and distress. Every species, with its extraordinary qualities and environmental job, adds to the profound profundity of the dance. The close to home reverberation fills in as a strong inspiration for preservation, encouraging society to recognize the natural worth of each "note" in the orchestra of life and to pursue saving the magnificence and variety that enhance our planet.

7. **Termination's Unheard Ensemble:**
   Termination, the quiet director of the "Last Request Dance," organizes an unheard ensemble of vanishing. As species evaporate, their songs are lost, their natural commitments quieted. The unheard ensemble of eradication is a frightful update that once an animal groups is gone, its novel job and importance in the biological story are unavoidably deleted. This highlights the irreversible idea of annihilation and the basic to act

conclusively to forestall the elimination of species at present trapped in their last supplication dance.

8. **Protection as a Dance of Trust:**
In the midst of the powerful stories of the "Last Request Dance," preservation arises as a dance of trust. Protection endeavors become a movement that looks to invert the direction of decline, giving a life saver to jeopardized species. The dance of trust includes environment reclamation, hostage reproducing programs, local area commitment, and worldwide coordinated effort — all pointed toward offering species an opportunity to rejoin the continuous ensemble of life. Protection turns into a resonating confirmation that humankind can assume a part in rejuvenating the dance of biodiversity.

9. **The Earnestness of the Last Development:**
The "Last Request Dance" crescendos in the criticalness of the last development, stressing that there's no time to waste. The open door to save imperiled species is shutting quickly. The direness highlights the requirement for prompt and coordinated activity to address the main drivers of biodiversity misfortune and execute compelling protection procedures. The last development is a require an aggregate obligation to focus on biodiversity preservation and guarantee that the dance of life perseveres for people in the future.

10. **A Movement of Variation:**
The dance of variation turns into a critical part of the "Last Supplication Dance." Species confronting termination should adjust to changing natural circumstances, looking for new living spaces, changing ways of behaving, or changing regenerative techniques. The movement of transformation mirrors the flexibility of life despite difficulty.
Notwithstanding, the quick speed of human-prompted changes presents extraordinary difficulties, and a few animal varieties wind up in a test of skill and endurance, endeavoring to adjust before their dance closes.

11. **The Interconnected Movement:**
The interconnectedness of species and biological systems highlights the cooperative movement of the "Last Request Dance." The endurance of one animal types frequently relies upon the presence and associations of others. The many-sided snare of biological connections requires an amicable movement that thinks about the necessities, everything being equal. This interconnected dance underscores the association of species and the need of all encompassing protection moves toward that address the more extensive biological setting.

12. **A Developing Movement:**
The "Last Request Dance" unfurls as an advancing movement, reflecting the unique idea of environments. Protection techniques should adjust

and advance because of new data, arising dangers, and changing natural elements. The developing movement underlines the requirement for adaptability, advancement, and a readiness to embrace new methodologies in the continuous work to safeguard biodiversity and support the dance of life.

13. **The Inconspicuous Artists:**

The similitude of the "Last Supplication Dance" stretches out past the charming megafauna and leader species, focusing on the frequently neglected and concealed artists in the biological troupe. Microorganisms, bugs, parasites, and other less obvious creatures assume crucial parts in the dance of life. The inconspicuous artists feature the significance of perceiving and safeguarding the full range of biodiversity, from the grand to the tiny.

14. **A Dance of Concurrence:**

The "Last Supplication Dance" is likewise a dance of conjunction, underlining the significance of agreeable connections among people and the normal world. Preservation includes tracking down ways for human social orders to coincide reasonably with biodiversity, recognizing that the prosperity of both is unpredictably entwined. The dance of concurrence moves us to reexamine our relationship with nature and embrace rehearses that consider the thriving of different living things.

15. **The Dance of Flexibility:**

Flexibility turns into a vital subject in the "Last Supplication Dance," as species endeavor to endure natural difficulties and return from the edge of termination. The dance of flexibility highlights the intrinsic limit of life to adjust, recuperate, and endure. Preservation endeavors that improve the versatility of biological systems and species add to a more hearty and persevering through dance of life.

16. **Preservation as a Social Dance:**

Preservation changes into a social dance, mirroring the qualities, convictions, and customs of social orders all over the planet. Native information, neighborhood rehearses, and social viewpoints shape the movement of protection. Perceiving and regarding different social commitments to the dance of biodiversity cultivates a comprehensive and comprehensive way to deal with protection that lines up with the upsides of various networks.

17. **A Call for Preservation Harmonies:**

All in all, the similitude of the "Last Supplication Dance" fills in as a strong call for protection harmonies that reverberate across the globe. It prompts mankind to pay attention to the quiet cries of jeopardized species, to perceive the interconnectedness of all living things, and to go about as humane choreographers in the continuous dance of biodiversity. The dire supplication of imperiled species is an encouragement to participate in the preservation dance — an aggregate undertaking that commends the excellence, variety, and flexibility of the normal world. In answering this call, mankind has the potential chance to become stewards of a flourishing and getting through orchestra, guaranteeing that the dance of life keeps on unfurling with elegance and imperativeness.

8.1 A closer look at species on the brink of extinction.

A more critical glance at species near the very edge of elimination uncovers an embroidery of environmental stories, logical difficulties, and dire preservation goals. This investigation digs into the complexities of species wavering on the edge of endurance, inspecting the elements driving their downfall, the biological outcomes of their likely misfortune, and the multi-layered endeavors expected to pull them back from the verge. From charming megafauna to subtle microorganisms, every species on the slope of elimination addresses a novel part in the unfurling story of biodiversity under danger.

1. **The Alluring Essences of Emergency:**
   Alluring megafauna, with their notable and frequently significant status, become the essences of the emergency encompassing species near the very edge of annihilation. From glorious tigers and elephants to cryptic rhinoceroses and polar bears, these species catch public consideration and bring areas of strength for out opinions. The situation of these charming countenances fills in as an energizing point for worldwide protection endeavors, featuring the interconnectedness between their endurance and the soundness of whole environments.

2. **Minuscule Wonders:**
   Nonetheless, a more critical gander at species near the precarious edge of elimination uncovers that the emergency stretches out past the charming countenances to incorporate infinitesimal wonders that frequently get away from the public eye. Bugs, growths, microorganisms, and other little however environmentally huge life forms assume significant parts in keeping up with the equilibrium of biological systems. The downfall of these unnoticeable species, however less noticeable, can have significant and flowing impacts on environmental cycles, underscoring the significance of a comprehensive way to deal with preservation.

3. **The Human Impression:**
   At the core of the emergency lies the irrefutable effect of the human impression. Environment obliteration, environmental change, contamination, overexploitation, and other anthropogenic exercises arise as essential drivers driving species to the edge of elimination. The tireless extension of human exercises into normal natural surroundings disturbs

the sensitive harmony that supports biodiversity, speeding up the rate at which species face the danger of vanishing from the planet.

4. **The Cascading type of influence of Environment Misfortune:**
Environment misfortune stands apart as a basic figure the stories of species near the very edge of eradication. As normal scenes surrender to urbanization, farming, and framework improvement, species lose their homes and the assets fundamental for their endurance. The cascading type of influence of living space misfortune resonates through biological systems, upsetting environmental connections, lessening accessible specialties, and delivering species more powerless against extra stressors.

5. **Environmental Change as a Guilty party:**
The approaching apparition of environmental change further fuels the difficulties looked by species near the very edge of annihilation. Increasing temperatures, modified precipitation examples, and outrageous climate occasions disturb territories and push species past their versatile cutoff points. The confuse between species' biological prerequisites and the changing environment represents an imposing danger, requiring versatile techniques and protection mediations to relieve the effects of a warming world.

6. **Overexploitation and Impractical Practices:**
Overexploitation, driven by the interest for assets, represents an immediate danger to numerous species. Hunting, fishing, logging, and the unlawful untamed life exchange add to the fast decay of populaces, especially for species with financial worth or those sought after in illicit businesses. Impractical practices, driven by transient additions disregarding long haul results, highlight the requirement for capable asset the board and protection estimates that focus on the prosperity of biological systems.

7. **Intrusive Species and Illness:**
Intrusive species and illnesses arise as quiet trespassers, further testing the versatility of species near the very edge of annihilation. Non-local species, presented deliberately or unintentionally, can outcompete local greenery, upset biological equilibriums, and add to the downfall of native species. Sicknesses, at times exacerbated by living space fracture and stress, can wreck populaces and drive weak species nearer to eradication, requiring careful checking and intercession.

8. **Natural Results of Decline:**
The decay of species near the very edge of termination conveys significant environmental outcomes that stretch out past the prompt loss of individual species. The perplexing snare of collaborations inside environments unwinds as central participants vanish, setting off trophic fountains, modified supplement cycles, and disturbances in biological system administrations. The biological outcomes highlight the interconnectedness of

species and the sensitive equilibrium expected for environments to work reasonably.

9. **Preservation Difficulties and Problems:**
Preservation endeavors for species near the very edge of eradication are laden with difficulties and moral situations. The direness of the circumstance frequently conflicts with the intricacies of carrying out powerful preservation systems.

Hostage rearing projects, renewed introduction endeavors, and living space reclamation drives wrestle with issues like hereditary variety, sickness transmission, and the expected unseen side-effects of intercession. Traditionalists explore a fragile way, meaning to figure out some kind of harmony between saving species and keeping up with the biological trustworthiness of their natural surroundings.

10. **The Job of Preservation Foundations:**
Preservation foundations, going from nearby philanthropies to worldwide associations, assume a crucial part in tending to the emergency of species near the very edge of elimination. These establishments lead research, carry out protection programs, bring issues to light, and backer for strategies that defend biodiversity. Cooperative endeavors between legislative organizations, NGOs, and nearby networks become fundamental for creating and executing complete protection designs that address the main drivers of species decline.

11. **Local area Commitment and Native Information:**
Comprehensive preservation techniques perceive the significance of local area commitment and native information in protecting species and their environments. Nearby people group frequently occupy regions wealthy in biodiversity and have significant customary information about existing together with nature. Coordinating native viewpoints into protection endeavors upgrades the viability of drives as well as advances a more evenhanded and economical way to deal with biodiversity preservation.

12. **The Job of Innovation in Preservation:**
Mechanical progressions offer new devices and philosophies for tending to the difficulties of species near the precarious edge of elimination. Remote detecting, DNA investigation, satellite following, and computerized reasoning add to more precise checking, evaluation, and the board of jeopardized populaces. The combination of innovation in protection endeavors upgrades the accuracy and proficiency of mediations, giving desire to improved results in the test of skill and endurance.

13. **Lawful Structures and Strategy Backing:**
The foundation and requirement of strong legitimate structures arise as basic parts in the battle to safeguard species near the very edge of termination. Peaceful accords, public regulations, and territorial strategies

give the legitimate framework to protection endeavors. Backing for more grounded ecological guidelines, territory security, and hostile to poaching measures becomes fundamental in molding approaches that focus on biodiversity protection and reasonable asset the board.

14. **The Moral Basic of Preservation:**
At its center, the preservation of species near the very edge of eradication is a moral goal.
Perceiving the inherent worth of every species, regardless of its utility to people, underscores the ethical obligation to forestall their elimination. The moral elements of preservation require a change in cultural qualities, empowering a more profound appreciation for the interconnectedness of life and the ethical obligation to go about as stewards of the planet.

15. **Preservation Examples of overcoming adversity:**
In the midst of the difficulties and emergencies, preservation examples of overcoming adversity offer encouraging signs. Occasions where coordinated endeavors have prompted the recuperation of species once near the precarious edge of annihilation show the versatility of nature and the viability of vital preservation intercessions. From the California condor to the dark footed ferret, these examples of overcoming adversity highlight the potential for positive change when networks, legislatures, and progressives team up with devotion and resolve.

16. **A Call for Worldwide Collaboration:**
The direness of the circumstance calls for exceptional worldwide participation in tending to the emergency of species near the precarious edge of annihilation. The interconnected idea of biological systems and the transboundary developments of numerous species require worldwide coordinated effort. A unified front against the drivers of biodiversity misfortune, combined with shared liability and assets, becomes basic in protecting the variety of life on The planet.

17. **The Convergence of Protection and Environment Activity:**
Perceiving the diversity of protection and environment activity becomes vital in tending to the difficulties looked by species near the precarious edge of elimination. Both environmental change and biodiversity misfortune are interconnected emergencies with shared main drivers. Moderating environmental change, progressing to economical practices, and safeguarding biodiversity meet as essential parts of an all encompassing way to deal with guaranteeing the endurance of species and the versatility of biological systems.

18. **A Future Changed by Preservation Decisions:**

All in all, a more critical gander at species near the very edge of termination uncovers a story that requests our consideration, empathy, and definitive activity. decisions today, with regards to preservation endeavors, feasible practices, and worldwide collaboration, will shape the fate of biodiversity.

The multifaceted dance of species, from the appealling to the tiny, mirrors the interconnected ensemble of life, and our job as stewards includes protecting this orchestra for the prosperity of the planet and people in the future. Despite difficulties, vulnerabilities, and moral problems, the basic to act isn't simply a call to safeguard individual species however to save the complex, interconnected dance that supports life on The planet.

8.2 Stories of those hanging on by a thread and the critical interventions required.

Accounts of species barely holding on summon a significant story of strength, weakness, and the earnest requirement for basic mediations to forestall their slide into elimination. This investigation dives into the stories of species on the verge, featuring their battles, the intricate snare of dangers they face, and the urgent mediations expected to guarantee their endurance. From the famous to the less popular, these accounts highlight the sensitive harmony among presence and elimination and the moral basic to go about as stewards of biodiversity.

1. **Famous Goliaths Wrestling with Annihilation:**
   The tales of famous monsters, like the African elephant and the Sumatran orangutan, encapsulate the difficulties looked by species barely surviving. These superb animals, mainstays of their biological systems, stand up to a flood of dangers going from territory misfortune and fracture to poaching and human-natural life struggle. The predicament of famous goliaths fills in as a distinct update that even species with far reaching verifiable populaces are not resistant to the hazards of termination despite tenacious human exercises.

2. **The Quiet Battle of Overlooked Species:**
   Past the focus on alluring megafauna, overlooked species discreetly persevere through their quiet battle on the incline of termination. Microorganisms, bugs, creatures of land and water, and endless different living beings assume significant parts in keeping up with environmental equilibrium. The decay of these frequently ignored species can have significant ramifications for whole biological systems, testing how we might interpret interconnectedness and highlighting the requirement for comprehensive protection endeavors that focus on the conservation of biodiversity in the entirety of its structures.

3. **Creatures of land and water: An Orchestra in Danger:**
   The story of creatures of land and water unfurls as an orchestra in danger,

with numerous species wavering on the edge. Chytrid parasite, territory misfortune, and environmental change make a dangerous crescendo compromising these delicate animals.

Creatures of land and water, filling in as signs of ecological wellbeing, add to bug control, supplement cycling, and clinical examination. The delicacy of their reality highlights the multifaceted equilibrium expected to support biodiversity, and their accounts feature the desperation of designated mediations to protect their novel commitments to environments.

4. **Flying predators: Taking off on the Edge:**
Accounts of flying predators, when taking off gloriously across the skies, presently portray a story of weakness. Raptors face dangers like living space annihilation, harming from pesticides, and unlawful hunting. The downfall of these birds signals natural irregular characteristics as well as focuses to the requirement for severe preservation measures to safeguard their environments and alleviate the effects of human exercises. Mediations, including natural surroundings reclamation and the guideline of destructive substances, become basic to guarantee these flying trackers keep on gracing the skies.

5. **Marine Wonders Confronting the Chasm:**
Underneath the waves, marine wonders face an alternate arrangement of provokes that drive them to the edge. Coral reefs, frequently alluded to as the rainforests of the ocean, are jeopardized by coral blanching, overfishing, and sea fermentation. Famous species like the ocean turtle and the vaquita, a little porpoise, are setbacks from horrendous fishing practices and territory debasement. The narratives of these marine species highlight the interconnected dangers that request comprehensive preservation techniques and worldwide participation to safeguard the delicate biological systems they occupy.

6. **The Polar Predicament: Cold and Antarctic Environments in Danger:**
The polar locales, once viewed as remote and immaculate, presently take the stand concerning the significant effects of environmental change and human exercises. Polar bears, symbolic of the Icy, face the test of disappearing ocean ice, influencing their hunting grounds and prey accessibility. Additionally, penguins in the Antarctic fight with moving ice designs and modified food networks. The polar predicament emphasizes the worldwide idea of protection endeavors and the basic job of alleviating environmental change to get the eventual fate of these famous species and the interesting biological systems they occupy.

7. **Jeopardized Plants: Watchmen of Biodiversity:**
The predicament of jeopardized plants, frequently eclipsed by the magnetic fauna, unfurls as a quiet emergency with extensive results. Many plant species face territory obliteration, obtrusive species, and

environmental change. As the underpinning of earthbound biological systems, imperiled plants assume an essential part in giving food, safe house, and oxygen.

The tales of these herbal gatekeepers underscore the requirement for designated protection intercessions, including living space rebuilding, seed banking, and public mindfulness, to guarantee the endurance of the natural spine of biodiversity.

8. **The Interconnected Trap of Dangers:**
Species barely holding on stand up to a complicated and interconnected snare of dangers that intensify the difficulties of preservation. Territory misfortune, environmental change, contamination, intrusive species, and direct double-dealing structure a tangled network that disintegrates the strength of biological systems. Understanding and tending to this trap of dangers require thorough preservation moves toward that incorporate logical information, local area commitment, and strategy backing to make successful and manageable arrangements.

9. **Protection Intercessions: From Emergency to Trust:**
Basic intercessions arise as encouraging signs in the midst of the stories of species confronting unavoidable eradication. Preservation endeavors incorporate a range of methodologies, including natural surroundings security, rebuilding, hostage reproducing projects, and local area based drives. The examples of overcoming adversity of species that have been pulled back from the edge, like the California condor and the dark footed ferret, represent the positive results feasible through designated and decided preservation intercessions.

10. **Environment Insurance and Rebuilding:**
At the very front of basic mediations is the basic to secure and reestablish natural surroundings. Protecting regular scenes, making natural life passages, and restoring debased biological systems are crucial activities to furnish species with the space and assets fundamental for their endurance. Preservation drives that emphasis on getting and restoring territories contribute not exclusively to the recuperation of individual species yet additionally to the general wellbeing and versatility of environments.

11. **Hostage Reproducing and Renewed introduction Projects:**
Hostage reproducing and renewed introduction programs assume a vital part in protecting species from the edge of termination. Preservationists influence hostage rearing offices to engender imperiled species in controlled conditions, guaranteeing their hereditary variety and regenerative achievement. Renewed introduction programs then, at that point, intend to once again introduce these people once more into their regular environments, offering another opportunity for endurance and building up waning populaces.

12. **Local area Based Protection:**
The consideration of neighborhood networks in preservation drives becomes fundamental for the achievement and supportability of mediations. Perceiving the crucial job networks play as stewards of regular assets, local area based protection engages neighborhood occupants to effectively partake in shielding their surroundings. This approach advances a feeling of pride as well as adjusts protection endeavors to the requirements and goals of the networks living close by imperiled species.

13. **Logical Exploration and Observing:**
Logical examination and observing act as basic support points in the domain of basic mediations. Grasping the natural necessities, conduct, and populace elements of imperiled species is fundamental for forming compelling preservation methodologies. Cutting edge innovations, like satellite following, DNA examination, and remote detecting, improve the accuracy of observing endeavors, giving important information to direct protection navigation.

14. **Strategy Backing and Lawful Securities:**
Backing for more grounded natural approaches and legitimate securities is fundamental in the battle against species decline. Powerful legitimate systems, both at public and worldwide levels, give the fundamental devices to control exercises that present dangers to biodiversity. Support endeavors expect to fortify existing regulations, close requirement holes, and lay out new insurances to guarantee that species on the edge benefit from legitimate protections that focus on their endurance.

15. **Instructive Drives and Public Mindfulness:**
Instructive drives and public mindfulness crusades act as impetuses for encouraging a preservation ethos inside society. Bringing issues to light about the situation of species on the verge makes educated and connected with networks that are bound to help preservation measures. Natural instruction, outreach projects, and media crusades add to a more extensive social shift toward esteeming biodiversity and perceiving the interconnectedness of all living things.

16. **Corporate Obligation and Manageable Practices:**
Tending to the underlying drivers of species decline requires corporate obligation and the reception of manageable practices. Organizations and businesses assume a critical part in driving territory obliteration, contamination, and asset double-dealing.

By embracing harmless to the ecosystem works on, taking on practical stock chains, and supporting protection drives, organizations add to moderating their effect on biodiversity and adjusting their tasks to biological stewardship.

17. **Worldwide Coordinated effort: A Worldwide Goal:**
    The worldwide idea of biodiversity decline highlights the requirement for global coordinated effort. Transboundary species, transitory examples, and the interconnectedness of environments request facilitated endeavors on a worldwide scale. Peaceful accords, like the Show on Natural Variety, give structures to cooperative activity, accentuating the common obligation of countries to secure and save the variety of life on The planet.

18. **Moral Contemplations in Preservation:**
    Implanted inside basic mediations are moral contemplations that shape decisions in preservation rehearses. Inquiries of how and when to mediate, the likely outcomes of intercessions, and the moral treatment of individual creatures all add to the developing talk on moral protection. Adjusting the basic to save species with the moral obligation to stay away from accidental damage turns into a core value in the turn of events and execution of protection methodologies.

19. **From Emergency to Trust: The Basic for Pressing Activity:**

All in all, the tales of species barely holding on present a piercing story that explores the domains of emergency and trust. The complicated snare of dangers they face requires pressing and conclusive activity. Basic mediations, spreading over natural surroundings security, hostage rearing, local area commitment, and global cooperation, give a guide to tending to the difficulties of species decline.

The basic to go about as stewards of biodiversity isn't just a logical need yet an ethical obligation that rises above individual species and resounds with the characteristic worth of life on The planet. The stories of those barely holding on coax mankind to set out on an aggregate excursion of protection, perceiving that in defending the variety of life, we save the complicated and interconnected ensemble that supports our planet.

8.3 Examining the ethical and moral dimensions of letting a species disappear.

Inspecting the moral and moral elements of allowing an animal groups to vanish uncovers a mind boggling exchange of values, obligations, and results that reach out past biological contemplations. The looming elimination of an animal varieties prompts significant inquiries concerning mankind's moral commitments to the normal world, the ethical ramifications of our activities, and the more extensive effect of losing biodiversity. As we dive into these aspects, we face moral problems, investigate the inherent worth of every species, and wrestle with the interconnectedness of life on The planet.

1. **The Characteristic Worth of Biodiversity:**
   At the center of the moral assessment lies the acknowledgment of the characteristic worth of biodiversity. Every species, no matter what its utility to people, adds to the perplexing woven artwork of life. From minute creatures to magnetic megafauna, each living element assumes a part in biological cycles, supports environments, and enhances the planet's variety. Recognizing the natural worth of biodiversity lays out an establishment for moral contemplations, stressing that the presence of an animal types holds esteem free of its utility to humankind.

2. **The Moral Basic to Protect:**
   The moral basic to protect species emerges from an acknowledgment of our job as stewards of the Earth. Human exercises, including natural surroundings annihilation, environmental change, and contamination, have become essential drivers of biodiversity misfortune. Considering our effect on the normal world, there arises a moral obligation to relieve the effects of our activities and endeavor to protect species near the very edge of elimination. This basic lines up with moral systems that underscore the significance of ecological stewardship and the ethical obligation to protect the extravagance of life for present and people in the future.

3. **The Cascading type of influence of Eradication:**
   The moral and moral aspects stretch out past the destiny of individual species to the more extensive results of their annihilation. The interconnectedness of environments implies that the deficiency of one animal groups can set off a cascading type of influence, influencing others in a flowing way. The elimination of a key pollinator, for instance, can disturb plant generation, influencing herbivores and hunters further up the pecking order. Understanding the potential expanding influences highlights the moral basic to forestall the deficiency of species and keep up with the mind boggling balance that supports natural agreement.

4. **The Ethical Load of Human Activities:**
   The ethical load of human activities in driving species to annihilation prompts reflection on the moral components of our decisions. Living space obliteration, overexploitation, and environmental change, to a great extent credited to human exercises, contribute fundamentally to the decay of species. Perceiving the ethical ramifications of our activities includes a basic assessment of the qualities supporting cultural standards, financial frameworks, and asset use. Moral contemplations welcome a reexamination of our relationship with the normal world and a guarantee to rehearses that line up with biological supportability.

5. **Anthropocentrism versus Biocentrism:**
   The moral assessment digs into the pressure among anthropocentrism and biocentrism — two differentiating viewpoints that shape our relationship

with nature. Anthropocentrism focuses on human interests, frequently seeing nature as an asset to be taken advantage of for human advantage. Interestingly, biocentrism stretches out moral thought to every single living being, perceiving the inborn worth of non-human substances. The moral discussion spins around finding some kind of harmony between human requirements and the freedoms of different species, featuring the test of accommodating human-centric inclinations with the ethical basic to regard the independence of non-human existence.

6. **The Job of Consciousness and Moral Thought:**
The moral assessment extends as contemplations of consciousness become an integral factor. Conscious creatures, fit for encountering delight, torment, and a scope of feelings, inspire more grounded moral thought. While numerous species show complex ways of behaving and mental capacities, the moral inquiry of whether awareness ought to direct our ethical commitments stays open. The discussion explores the ethical obligations toward species with shifting levels of consciousness and brings up issues about the models used to decide the ethical load of various creatures.

7. **The Moral Quandary of Mediation:**
The moral situation encompassing mediation despite species decline is a focal part of the assessment. Preservation endeavors, including hostage rearing, territory reclamation, and renewed introduction programs, include human impedance in normal cycles. The moral elements of these mediations include inquiries concerning the possible potentially negative side-effects, the impedance with normal determination, and the ethical power to pursue choices for the benefit of different species. Finding some kind of harmony between non-interventionist morals and the basic to forestall eradication turns into a complex moral test.

8. **Preservation Emergency and Hard decisions:**
Preservation emergency, an idea established in the designation of restricted assets to species with the most elevated probability of recuperation, presents one more layer of moral intricacy. When confronted with scant assets and various species on the verge, traditionalists should settle on hard choices about where to coordinate their endeavors. The moral quandary lies in figuring out which species are considered more significant or have a higher opportunity of effective recuperation, bringing up issues about the standards used to focus on mediations and the moral ramifications of possibly allowing specific species to vanish.

9. **Moral Contemplations in De-Elimination Endeavors:**
Progresses in hereditary advancements make the way for de-eradication endeavors, bringing up moral issues about the revival of terminated species. The possibility of bringing back species through cloning or

hereditary control presents moral contemplations with respect to the expected outcomes, the biological effect, and the moral supports for such intercessions. De-elimination endeavors brief a reexamination of our relationship with the past, the obligations related with species restoration, and the moral components of assuming a part in the revival of wiped out organic entities.

10. **The Intergenerational Morals of Biodiversity:**
The moral assessment reaches out across ages, presenting the idea of intergenerational morals. Protecting biodiversity is a moral commitment that rises above the current second, conveying suggestions for the prosperity of people in the future. decisions today, in regards to preservation rehearses, asset use, and ecological strategies, shape the inheritance gave to the individuals who will acquire the planet. Intergenerational morals underscore the obligation to consider the requirements and interests of people in the future in the moral math of allowing an animal groups to vanish.

11. **Native Viewpoints on Biodiversity:**
Native viewpoints give important experiences into the moral contemplations encompassing biodiversity. Numerous native societies view nature as interconnected and consider the prosperity of biological systems fundamental to their own. Native information stresses the significance of amicable associations with the regular world and offers moral structures that line up with supportable practices. Perceiving and regarding these points of view becomes fundamental in cultivating moral protection moves toward that honor the variety of values and perspectives.

12. **Moral Commercialization and Supportable Practices:**
Individual decisions, especially in the domain of commercialization, convey moral ramifications for biodiversity. Moral commercialization accentuates settling on decisions that line up with natural maintainability, supporting organizations and practices that focus on preservation and mindful asset the board. The moral components of purchaser decisions reach out to contemplations of territory safeguarding, the effect of creation processes on environments, and the moral obligations related with utilization designs.

13. **The Worldwide House and Shared Liability:**
The moral assessment extends to envelop the idea of the worldwide center — shared assets that rise above public limits. Biodiversity, existing as a worldwide hall, requests shared liability in its safeguarding. Worldwide cooperation, the sharing of information and assets, and aggregate endeavors to address worldwide drivers of biodiversity misfortune become moral goals in perceiving the interconnected idea of environments and the common destiny of species across borders.

14. **The Moral Commitment to Future Revelations:**
The possibility of unseen species adds a layer of moral commitment to biodiversity safeguarding. Numerous species, particularly in biodiversity areas of interest, stay obscure to science. The moral basic to safeguard these territories and environments isn't just a promise to known animal groups yet additionally an acknowledgment of the potential for future logical revelations. The moral commitment to safeguard biodiversity reaches out to the yet-to-be-uncovered fortunes of the normal world.

15. **Training, Compassion, and Moral Change:**
Training arises as an integral asset in molding moral viewpoints on biodiversity. Encouraging compassion towards different species, figuring out environmental interconnectedness, and ingraining a feeling of obligation for preservation add to moral change. Ecological schooling turns into a foundation in developing a cultural ethos that values biodiversity, perceives the honest convictions related with species safeguarding, and engages people to settle on moral decisions in their collaborations with the normal world.

16. **The Outcomes of Inaction:**
Inspecting the moral and moral elements of allowing an animal categories to vanish requires a thought of the results of inaction. The deficiency of biodiversity not just reduces the magnificence and intricacy of the normal world yet in addition compromises environment administrations, disturbs biological equilibriums, and imperils the prosperity of human networks. Moral contemplations stretch out past individual species to envelop the more extensive results of a world devastated by the vanishing of its different living things.

17. **A Call for Moral Preservation Initiative:**

All in all, the moral and moral components of allowing an animal groups to vanish challenge mankind to rethink its relationship with the normal world. The acknowledgment of the natural worth of biodiversity, the moral basic to protect, and the thought of outcomes past biological domains highlight the requirement for moral preservation authority.

Exploring the moral intricacies includes a pledge to capable asset the executives, economical practices, and aggregate endeavors to address the underlying drivers of biodiversity misfortune. The call for moral preservation initiative entices mankind to go about as scrupulous stewards of the Earth, perceiving the ethical commitment to shield the wealth of life for present and people in the future.

CHAPTER 9

Conservation Harmony

Preservation Concordance addresses the fragile and complicated orchestra of endeavors pointed toward protecting biodiversity, supporting biological systems, and cultivating an agreeable concurrence among people and the regular world. This complete idea rises above simple preservation rehearses; it embodies a comprehensive methodology that interweaves natural, social, and moral contemplations. As we dig into the multi-layered layers of Protection Congruity, we explore the convergences of science, local area commitment, strategy backing, and the moral basic to figure out some kind of harmony that guarantees the progression of the World's different living things.

1. **The Biological Expressive dance:**
   At the core of Preservation Congruity lies the natural expressive dance — a movement that coordinates the communications between species, territories, and environments. This unpredictable dance unfurls across different scenes, from lavish rainforests to broad seas, with every species assuming an exceptional part.

   The preservation of biodiversity includes saving individual species as well as understanding and keeping up with the unique connections that structure the natural expressive dance. This requires a profound appreciation for the intricacy of environments and the acknowledgment that every species adds to the versatility and usefulness of the entirety.

2. **The Orchestra of Interconnectedness:**
   The orchestra of Preservation Congruity resounds with the key standard of interconnectedness. Biological systems are unpredictable networks where each specie, regardless of how little or unnoticeable, plays a part to play. From the minuscule living beings in the dirt to the appealling hunters at the head of the pecking order, each adds to the equilibrium and usefulness of the environment. Preservation endeavors should embrace

the comprehension that disturbing one piece of this orchestra can re-sound all through the whole structure, influencing the dependability and soundness of the environment.

3. **Crossing over Science and Preservation:**
   At the front of Preservation Concordance is the joining of logical informa-tion with protection rehearses. Researchers assume a significant part in disentangling the secrets of biodiversity, figuring out environmental cy-cles, and evaluating the effects of human exercises on the normal world. Overcoming any barrier between logical exploration and on-the-ground protection endeavors is fundamental for powerful and informed naviga-tion. Protection techniques grounded in thorough logical proof upgrade their accuracy and improve the probability of progress in safeguarding species and biological systems.

4. **Local area Commitment as a Melodic Component:**
   The melodic component of Protection Concordance reaches out to local area commitment — a feature in the ensemble of biodiversity conser-vation. Nearby people group, frequently living in closeness to regions wealthy in biodiversity, hold important information about their environ-ments. Including people group in protection drives takes advantage of this native insight as well as encourages a feeling of pride and obligation. Effective preservation methodologies perceive the cooperative connec-tion between nearby networks and their normal environmental factors, advancing an agreeable conjunction that benefits the two individuals and the climate.

5. **The Moral Suggestion:**
   Morals structure the suggestion that establishes the vibe for Preservation Concordance. Perceiving the inherent worth of every species, the ethical obligation to go about as stewards of the Earth, and the moral basic to save biodiversity guide the standards of preservation.
   The moral contemplations reach out to inquiries of mediation, the results of human activities on the normal world, and the all-encompassing moral obligation to people in the future. Preservation Agreement places morals at its center, underlining the requirement for mindful and principled ways to deal with defending the variety of life on The planet.

6. **Strategy and Administration as the Leading Stick:**
   The leading stick of Protection Concordance rests in the domain of strategy and administration. Compelling preservation requires steady lawful sys-tems, clear cut guidelines, and strong implementation components. Leg-islatures, worldwide bodies, and non-administrative associations assume the part of directors, arranging arrangements that energize economical practices, safeguard basic living spaces, and address the underlying driv-ers of biodiversity misfortune. The arrangement of strategies with the

standards of Protection Concordance guarantees a planned and effective exertion for a bigger scope.

7. **Manageable Practices: The Cadenced Establishment:**
Manageable practices structure the musical underpinning of Protection Congruity. Whether in horticulture, fisheries, or businesses, taking on rehearses that focus on natural supportability is pivotal. Practical asset the board, dependable utilization, and the decrease of natural impressions add to the cadenced steadiness of the protection orchestra. Protection Concordance requires a change in perspective toward rehearses that guarantee the drawn out wellbeing and essentialness of biological systems, perceiving the relationship of human prosperity and environmental respectability.

8. **Innovative Crescendos:**
Innovative progressions acquaint crescendos with the Preservation Congruity orchestra. Advancements in remote detecting, information examination, and checking innovations upgrade the accuracy and proficiency of protection endeavors. Satellite symbolism supports environment observing, DNA examination helps track jeopardized populaces, and computerized reasoning adds to prescient demonstrating. The combination of innovation enhances the ability to screen and answer changes in biodiversity, adding dynamic layers to the ensemble of preservation.

9. **Instructive Harmonies:**
Instructive drives create harmonies that resound across society, cultivating a comprehension of and obligation to Preservation Congruity. Ecological schooling, mindfulness missions, and effort programs assume essential parts in forming a protection ethos. By imparting an appreciation for nature, environmental interconnections, and the significance of biodiversity, instruction turns into a groundbreaking power that impacts individual and aggregate ways of behaving. Educated and engaged networks are fundamental members in the amicable ensemble of protection.

10. **Coordinated effort as a Binding together Ensemble:**
Coordinated effort arises as the binding together ensemble that unites different partners chasing Preservation Congruity. The difficulties of biodiversity misfortune are worldwide, requiring aggregate endeavors that rise above boundaries, trains, and interests. Legislatures, non-benefits, organizations, researchers, and neighborhood networks orchestrate their endeavors, perceiving that the ensemble of preservation is most effective when played as an aggregate piece. Joint effort cultivates the trading of information, assets, and mastery, making a unified front against the dangers to biodiversity.

11. **Versatile Flexibility as a Melodic Reaction:**
Despite natural changes and vulnerabilities, versatile strength turns into

a melodic reaction inside Protection Congruity. Environments, species, and protection methodologies should have the adaptability to adjust to advancing circumstances. This versatility includes recognizing that change is a consistent in the normal world and that protection rehearses should be versatile and responsive. Protection Congruity requires a comprehension of the unique idea of biological systems and a promise to cultivating strength despite progressing ecological difficulties.

12. **Preservation Money as the Supporting Bassline:**
The supporting bassline of Preservation Congruity is played by protection finance — a frequently overlooked at this point pivotal component. Subsidizing is fundamental for executing preservation drives, supporting exploration, and laying out safeguarded regions. The monetary help can emerge out of administrative spending plans, generosity, corporate ventures, and creative supporting instruments. A powerful bassline of protection finance guarantees the dependability and life span of the ensemble, giving the assets expected to address the complex difficulties of biodiversity safeguarding.

13. **Regarding Native Harmonies:**
Regarding and incorporating native points of view into protection rehearses contribute novel harmonies to the general orchestra of Preservation Concordance. Native people group frequently have conventional information, economical practices, and social qualities that line up with natural equilibrium. Perceiving and regarding these points of view enhances protection techniques as well as recognizes the authentic associations between native networks and their surroundings. Native harmonies offer a significant contrast that upgrades the variety and flexibility of the preservation ensemble.

14. **Metropolitan Environment: A Cutting edge Development:**
As urbanization speeds up, the cutting edge development of metropolitan environment arises as an unmistakable song inside Protection Concordance. Perceiving that a critical piece of the worldwide populace dwells in metropolitan regions, metropolitan environment investigates ways of coordinating nature into urban areas, making spaces that help biodiversity, give biological system administrations, and improve the prosperity of metropolitan occupants. Offsetting metropolitan improvement with environmental supportability turns into an agreeable undertaking that expects to fit human settlements with the regular world.

15. **Adjusting Preservation Concordance to Environmental Change:**
Environmental change presents a difficult beat shift in the preservation orchestra, requiring a transformation of Protection Concordance to new rhythms. Increasing temperatures, adjusted precipitation examples, and outrageous climate occasions request techniques that address the effects

of environmental change on biodiversity. Protection Congruity turns into a unique creation that integrates environment versatility, relief endeavors, and inventive answers for explore the difficulties presented by a quickly evolving environment.

16. **Preservation The travel industry: A Melodic Coalition:**
Protection the travel industry arises as a melodic collusion that fits financial exercises with biodiversity conservation. Economical and capable the travel industry rehearses add to nearby economies while advancing the protection of regular environments. Preservation the travel industry encourages an appreciation for biodiversity, upholds preservation drives monetarily, and makes impetuses for neighborhood networks to take part in the assurance of their regular legacy. This melodic collusion changes the travel industry from a likely danger to biodiversity into an agreeable power for protection.

17. **The Continuous Ensemble of Trust:**
Protection Congruity is definitely not a static structure however a continuous ensemble of trust that develops with the changing elements of the regular world and human social orders. It recognizes that difficulties continue, new dangers might arise, and arrangements should be versatile. The ensemble of trust moves proceeded with devotion to the safeguarding of biodiversity, perceiving that each note played adds to the overall tune of an amicable and strong planet.

18. **The Suggestion to People in the future:**

All in all, Preservation Concordance addresses the suggestion to people in the future — a guarantee to pass on a world wealthy in biodiversity, environmental equilibrium, and interconnectedness. The orchestra of protection includes the environmental expressive dance, the ensemble of interconnectedness, and the harmonies of science, local area commitment, strategy support, and morals. It reverberates with the rhythms of manageable practices, innovative crescendos, instructive harmonies, and the bringing together melody of coordinated effort.

Preservation Concordance is the melodic reaction of versatile strength, the supporting bassline of protection finance, and the regard for native harmonies. It embraces the cutting edge development of metropolitan environment, adjusts to environmental change, and partners with preservation the travel industry. As the continuous ensemble of trust, Preservation Concordance welcomes mankind to participate in the aggregate work to guarantee the congruity of life's different songs, making an amicable heritage for a long time into the future.

9.1 Highlighting successful conservation stories and the restoration of balance.

Featuring effective preservation stories and the rebuilding of equilibrium divulges a story of trust, versatility, and the groundbreaking force of human endeavors to defend biodiversity. These accounts reverberate as signals of accomplishment, displaying that, with commitment, development, and coordinated effort, it is feasible to turn around the direction of species decline and reestablish congruity to environments. As we investigate these stories of win, we dive into the methodologies and mediations that have demonstrated compelling, revealing insight into the potential for positive change and the basic to increase effective protection tries.

1. **The Surprising Recovery of the California Condor:**
   The tale of the California condor remains as a demonstration of the wonderful restoration of an animal groups once wavering near the precarious edge of elimination. By the late twentieth 100 years, just a small bunch of California condors stayed in the wild, their populaces obliterated by lead harming and living space annihilation. Traditionalists set out on an aggressive recuperation program, including hostage rearing, living space security, and fastidious checking. Through many years of resolute commitment, the California condor populace has bounced back, with fruitful renewed introductions into nature. This achievement highlights the adequacy of cooperative protection techniques, consolidating logical skill, public mindfulness, and legislative help.

2. **Wolves Return to Yellowstone: A Trophic Outpouring Released:**
   The renewed introduction of wolves to Yellowstone Public Park during the 1990s remains as a famous illustration of natural rebuilding and the significant effect of cornerstone species. The shortfall of wolves had permitted elk populaces to flood, prompting overgrazing of vegetation and flowing consequences for different species. The renewed introduction of wolves set off a trophic outpouring — a cascading type of influence through the food web. With decreased elk numbers, vegetation bounced back, helping beavers, birds, and even stream biological systems. This example of overcoming adversity features the complexities of biological equilibrium and the potential for species renewed introduction to reestablish concordance to environments.

3. **Coral Reefs Strength in the Phoenix Islands:**
   In the midst of the worldwide emergency of coral reef decline, the Phoenix Islands in the focal Pacific recount an account of strength and viable protection. Assigned as a marine safeguarded region, the Phoenix Islands Safeguarded Region (PIPA) turned into a shelter for coral reefs confronting dangers, for example, environmental change and overfishing. Severe protection measures, remembering fishing limitations and a boycott for business extraction, permitted the reefs to recuperate. The outcome has

been a resurgence of marine life, lively coral networks, and a diagram for feasible marine preservation. The outcome in the Phoenix Islands underlines the crucial job of safeguarded regions in permitting environments to bounce back and reestablish harmony.

4. **Once more, the Bald Eagle Takes off: DDT Boycott and Natural surroundings Insurance:**
The recuperation of the bald eagle, the famous image of the US, addresses a triumph against the staggering impacts of the pesticide DDT. Boundless utilization of DDT had prompted diminishing eggshells, causing regenerative disappointment in bald eagle populaces. The restriction on DDT and deliberate endeavors to safeguard hawk territories made ready for a wonderful rebound. The bald eagle was eliminated from the imperiled species list in 2007, denoting a preservation example of overcoming adversity established in administrative activity, natural surroundings protection, and public mindfulness crusades.

5. **The Oryx Protection Progress in Oman:**
The Middle Eastern oryx, a desert gazelle, confronted impending elimination in the wild due to overhunting and environment debasement in Oman. Accordingly, an exhaustive protection program was started, including hostage rearing, environment reclamation, and severe enemy of poaching measures.
This coordinated methodology prompted a critical bounce back in the Bedouin oryx populace, and the species was effectively once again introduced into its local living space. The Omani oryx preservation achievement fills in as a model for animal varieties recuperation in parched conditions, exhibiting the viability of joining protection science with local area contribution.

6. **The Striking Rebound of the Iberian Lynx:**
The Iberian lynx, one of the world's most imperiled cats, confronted a critical circumstance with lessening populaces and a contracting natural surroundings in Spain and Portugal. An engaged preservation exertion, including hostage rearing projects, territory rebuilding, and prey the executives, reversed the situation for this slippery feline. Through coordinated endeavors, the Iberian lynx populace has seen a huge increment, offering a good omen for the species' endurance. This example of overcoming adversity highlights the significance of versatile protection systems customized to the particular necessities of imperiled species.

7. **The Humpback Whale's Excursion from Hazard to Assurance:**
The humpback whale, once chased extremely close to eradication for its lard and oil, has encountered a surprising recuperation following global preservation endeavors. The ban on business whaling, laid out by the Worldwide Whaling Commission in 1986, assumed a critical part

in safeguarding humpback whale populaces. Resulting preservation measures, for example, the assignment of marine safeguarded regions and guidelines to forestall transport strikes, further added to the species' resurgence. The humpback whale's excursion from risk to security shows the force of worldwide participation in moderating marine megafauna.

8. **The Recuperation of the Tasmanian Villain: Fighting a Lethal Illness:**
The Tasmanian villain confronted an extreme danger from a contagious malignant growth known as Demon Facial Cancer Illness (DFTD), which prompted a critical decrease in populaces across Tasmania. Preservationists answered with a multi-layered approach, including hostage rearing projects, infection the board techniques, and public mindfulness crusades. The fruitful foundation of sickness free populaces and the ID of safe people have offered trust for the drawn out endurance of this extraordinary marsupial. The tale of the Tasmanian fallen angel grandstands the strength of species despite arising dangers and the significance of versatile protection measures.

9. **The Bare Ibis Gets back to Europe's Skies:**
The Northern Bare Ibis, a transient bird animal groups, confronted eradication in Europe because of natural surroundings misfortune and human unsettling influence.
Traditionalists started a striking renewed introduction program that elaborate hand-raising chicks and directing them along their transitory course utilizing ultralight airplane. This inventive methodology planned to restore a self-supporting populace of the uncovered ibis. The venture, known as Waldrapp Group, has seen eminent accomplishment with the birds effectively relocating and reproducing in nature. The arrival of the Northern Bare Ibis to Europe's skies represents the inventive and cooperative arrangements that can reestablish harmony to biological systems.

10. **Buffalo Protection on the Incomparable Fields: From Close to Annihilation to Meandering Aimlessly:**
The American buffalo, a notable image of the Incomparable Fields, looked close to elimination in the nineteenth hundred years due to overhunting and living space misfortune. Preservation endeavors, including the foundation of safeguarded regions and the advancement of maintainable brushing rehearses, have permitted buffalo populaces to bounce back. Buffalo currently wander aimlessly in assigned regions, adding to environment wellbeing through their brushing ways of behaving. The progress of buffalo protection features the flexibility of an animal types whenever offered the chance to recuperate and the significance of reestablishing cornerstone species to their normal territories.

11. **The Kakapo Parrot's Battle Against Elimination:**
The Kakapo parrot, local to New Zealand, confronted the verge of

termination with just a modest bunch of people remaining. A devoted protection program, including serious hunter control, living space rebuilding, and a special rearing procedure, has prompted a sluggish yet consistent expansion in Kakapo numbers. The parrot's story embodies the difficulties and triumphs of rationing basically imperiled species on islands, where intrusive hunters represent a critical danger. The Kakapo's battle against elimination features the significance of versatile administration and long haul responsibility in species recuperation.

12. **The Resurrection of Monteverde Cloud Backwoods Save:**
The Monteverde Cloud Backwoods Save in Costa Rica remains as a signal of fruitful preservation and territory rebuilding. Once undermined by logging and rural extension, the save presently safeguards a different and flourishing cloud woodland biological system. Preservation endeavors zeroed in on reforestation, local area commitment, and maintainable the travel industry have changed Monteverde into a model for tropical timberland protection. The save's resurgence features the interconnectedness between preservation, local area association, and ecotourism in cultivating the rebuilding of adjusted biological systems.

13. **The Arrival of the European Buffalo: Rewilding Progress in Europe:**
The European buffalo, Europe's heaviest land warm blooded animal, confronted termination in the wild by the mid twentieth hundred years. Rewilding drives and deliberate preservation endeavors have prompted the fruitful restoration of European buffalo populaces in a few nations. The Buffalo Rewilding Project includes renewed introductions, natural surroundings reclamation, and local area commitment, adding to the rebuilding of huge herbivore elements in European biological systems. The arrival of the European buffalo epitomizes the potential for rewilding as a preservation methodology to reestablish harmony and biodiversity to debased scenes.

14. **The Pinta Island Turtle's Lazarus Second:**
The Pinta Island turtle, accepted to be terminated with the demise of Friendless George, encountered a Lazarus second with the disclosure of people with Pinta Island turtle hereditary qualities on an adjoining island. Protectionists started a rearing project to resuscitate the species, joining hereditary examination, hostage reproducing, and living space rebuilding. Despite the fact that difficulties persevere, the continuous endeavors to revive the Pinta Island turtle embody the assurance to turn around the effects of human-initiated species decline and reestablish harmony to island environments.

15. **The Recovery of the European Otter: A Riverine Example of overcoming adversity:**
The European otter, once seriously impacted by natural surroundings

misfortune, contamination, and human unsettling influence, has encountered a remarkable recovery across numerous European streams. Further developed water quality, environment rebuilding along riverbanks, and protection endeavors zeroed in on diminishing compound contaminations have added to the otter's recuperation. The arrival of otters to water biological systems connotes the rebuilding of equilibrium in riparian natural surroundings and features the potential for protection activities to switch the fortunes of species impacted by anthropogenic tensions.

16. **The Fruitful Fight Against Intrusive Species on Macquarie Island:**
Macquarie Island, a subantarctic island, confronted environmental pulverization because of obtrusive species like rodents and hares. Protectionists sent off an extensive destruction program to eliminate these trespassers, permitting local vegetation and seabird populaces to bounce back. The outcome in controlling obtrusive species on Macquarie Island fills in as a model for island reclamation endeavors worldwide, underscoring the significance of killing acquainted dangers with reestablish natural equilibrium and safeguard local biodiversity.

17. **The Red Kite's Recuperation in the Unified Realm: A Preservation Taking off Progress:**
The red kite, a flying predator local to the Unified Realm, confronted oppression and populace decline because of living space misfortune and unlawful harming. Preservation endeavors, including renewed introduction programs, environment security, and local area commitment, have prompted a critical recuperation of red kite populaces. Once more the progress of the red kite's protection epitomizes the positive results that outcome from coordinated endeavors to address different dangers all the while, making a scene where this magnificent raptor can take off openly.

18. **The Job of Native Preservation in Australia: Fire The board and Biodiversity:**
Native fire the board rehearses in Australia offer a convincing story of how customary biological information can add to preservation and the rebuilding of equilibrium. Native people group, with their profound association with the land, have long utilized controlled consuming to oversee scenes and advance biodiversity. Coordinating native fire the executives into contemporary preservation systems lessens the gamble of decimating fierce blazes as well as supports environment wellbeing, featuring the significance of integrating customary thinking into present day protection rehearses.

19. **The Protection Agreement of Ngorongoro Preservation Region: Adjusting Untamed life and Domesticated animals:**
The Ngorongoro Preservation Region in Tanzania represents the sensitive harmony between untamed life protection and conventional pastoralism.

This UNESCO World Legacy Site is home to assorted biological systems, including the notable Serengeti fields and the Ngorongoro Pit. Preservation endeavors here center around fitting the conjunction of untamed life and Maasai pastoralists. Economical land the executives, local area commitment, and natural life assurance add to the protection congruity of this novel region, showing that dwelling together among individuals and natural life is feasible with smart preparation and cooperative methodologies.

20. **The Uncovered Ibis Gets back to Europe's Skies:**

The Northern Bare Ibis, a transient bird animal groups, confronted elimination in Europe because of natural surroundings misfortune and human aggravation. Progressives started an intense renewed introduction program that elaborate hand-raising chicks and directing them along their transitory course utilizing ultralight airplane. This inventive methodology expected to restore a self-supporting populace of the uncovered ibis. The undertaking, known as Waldrapp Group, has seen remarkable accomplishment with the birds effectively moving and reproducing in nature. The arrival of the Northern Uncovered Ibis to Europe's skies epitomizes the inventive and cooperative arrangements that can reestablish harmony to biological systems.

All in all, the horde examples of overcoming adversity in preservation reverberation the versatility of the normal world and the extraordinary effect of human responsibility and creativity. These stories highlight the significance of versatile systems, local area contribution, strategy backing, and global cooperation in reestablishing harmony to environments and shielding biodiversity. As we commend these triumphs, they likewise act as a clarion call for proceeded with endeavors, perceiving that the reclamation of congruity is a continuous excursion. Through the aggregate coordination of fruitful preservation drives, we can seek to make an existence where the tales of species decline are supplanted with stories of recuperation, resurgence, and the getting through congruity of a biodiverse planet.

9.2 Examining the potential for human intervention to heal and protect ecosystems.

Inspecting the potential for human mediation to recuperate and safeguard biological systems digs into the perplexing interaction between human exercises, natural stewardship, and the reclamation of environmental equilibrium. In a time set apart by phenomenal ecological difficulties, investigating the manners by which human mediation can be saddled as a power for mending and security is critical. This assessment incorporates a range of mediations, from protection rehearses and supportable asset the board to reclamation drives and inventive innovations, with the general objective of encouraging a harmonious connection among humankind and the normal world.

1. **Protection Practices as Watchmen of Biodiversity:**
   At the front of human mediation in biological system recuperating is the reception of preservation rehearses intended to protect biodiversity. Safeguarded regions, untamed life stores, and marine safe-havens act as strongholds for imperiled species, giving shelters where normal cycles can unfurl undisturbed. Protection rehearses reach out past simple safeguarding, integrating territory reclamation, hostile to poaching endeavors, and local area commitment. The foundation of these safeguarded spaces not just guides in that frame of mind of compromised species yet additionally adds to the general flexibility of biological systems.

2. **Supportable Asset The board: Sustaining Congruity with Nature:**
   A significant part of human mediation includes embracing practical asset the executives as a core value. Offsetting human necessities with the limit of biological systems to recover guarantees the life span of imperative assets. Practices like maintainable ranger service, capable fisheries the board, and eco-accommodating farming embody the potential for people to coincide amicably with nature.
   By embracing approaches that focus on the drawn out strength of biological systems, we can moderate the effects of asset double-dealing and cultivate a reasonable connection among humankind and the climate.

3. **Environment Reclamation Drives: Resuscitating Corrupted Scenes:**
   Environment reclamation arises as a proactive intercession, expecting to switch the harm caused upon debased scenes. Whether through afforestation projects, wetland rebuilding, or rewilding drives, people have the ability to renew environments that have been modified by deforestation, contamination, or other anthropogenic exercises. Rebuilding restores biodiversity as well as upgrades environment administrations, like water decontamination, carbon sequestration, and soil ripeness. Looking at effective rebuilding projects gives experiences into the groundbreaking capability of purposeful human activity in mending and safeguarding biological systems.

4. **Native Information and Customary Practices: A Dependable Insight:**
   Native information and conventional practices offer a repository of tried and true insight that can direct compelling biological system mending. Native people group, profoundly associated with their surroundings, frequently have maintainable land the executives strategies, agroecological practices, and biodiversity protection techniques. Perceiving and regarding native viewpoints can illuminate contemporary protection systems,

guaranteeing that human intercessions line up with the mind boggling balance that native networks have kept up with for ages.

5. **Metropolitan Biology: Offsetting Urbanization with Natural Well-being:**
As urbanization speeds up worldwide, the idea of metropolitan environment arises as a critical field for human mediation in biological system mending. Planning urban areas with green spaces, executing supportable metropolitan preparation, and coordinating nature into metropolitan conditions add to relieving the biological impression of human settlements. Metropolitan biology stresses the concurrence of metropolitan turn of events and ecological wellbeing, showing how purposeful human intercessions can encourage versatile, nature-accommodating urban areas.

6. **Innovation as an Impetus for Preservation Development:**
In the period of fast mechanical progression, imaginative advances act as impetuses for preservation development. From satellite observing and drones for untamed life following to man-made consciousness for environmental demonstrating, innovation enhances the accuracy and effectiveness of human intercessions.
Looking at the job of innovation in biological system recuperating reveals insight into how state of the art devices can give continuous information, prescient examination, and novel answers for address ecological difficulties on a worldwide scale.

7. **Environmental Change Moderation and Variation: Exploring an Evolving Climate:**
Human mediation even with environmental change includes both alleviation and transformation methodologies. Moderation endeavors intend to diminish ozone harming substance outflows, changing towards environmentally friendly power sources, and carrying out maintainable practices. Variation methodologies center around improving the versatility of biological systems to endure the effects of an evolving environment. Looking at these mediations grandstands the diverse methodology expected to address perhaps of the most squeezing worldwide test and highlights the significance of human activity in forming an environment versatile future.

8. **Coordinated Water The board: Defending Oceanic Biological systems:**
Water, a basic asset for biological systems and human networks the same, requires deliberate intercession for compelling administration. Incorporated water the board includes procedures, for example, watershed security, reasonable water use, and rebuilding of amphibian natural surroundings. Inspecting fruitful water the board drives uncovers how human mediations can guarantee the accessibility of clean water, safeguard

sea-going biodiversity, and keep up with the sensitive equilibrium of freshwater environments.

9. **Preservation Money: Putting resources into the Eventual fate of Biodiversity:**

The monetary part of preservation, frequently ignored, assumes a significant part in human mediations for environment recuperating. Preservation finance includes coordinating assets towards protection projects, supporting exploration, and laying out reasonable subsidizing systems. Looking at the job of protection finance features the need of putting resources into the eventual fate of biodiversity, highlighting the monetary worth of flawless biological systems and the expense viability of precaution estimates over receptive reactions to ecological debasement.

10. **Local area Based Preservation: Engaging Nearby Stewardship:**

Engaging nearby networks as stewards of their regular assets shapes a crucial part of human mediation in environment mending. Local area based preservation draws in neighborhood information, values, and works on, encouraging a feeling of pride and obligation. Analyzing people group drove drives gives experiences into how enabling neighborhood partners can prompt more successful and manageable results, guaranteeing that human mediations line up with the requirements and goals of the networks straightforwardly associated with the biological systems being referred to.

11. **Preservation Instruction and Public Mindfulness: Encouraging Ecological Proficiency:**

An educated and connected with public is a strong problem solver in the domain of environment mending. Preservation schooling and public mindfulness crusades assume a significant part in molding perspectives, ways of behaving, and strategy choices. Looking at the effect of instructive mediations gives a more profound comprehension of how cultivating ecological education adds to a general public that qualities and effectively partakes in the security and rebuilding of biological systems.

12. **Strategy Support and Legitimate Systems: Forming Maintainable Practices:**

Human mediation in environment recuperating reaches out to the domain of strategy backing and the foundation of lawful systems. Successful natural strategies and guidelines give an establishment to maintainable works on, portraying limits and assumptions for ventures, states, and people. Looking at the job of strategy intercessions explains the potential for legitimate structures to impact conduct, drive advancement, and establish an empowering climate for environment assurance.

13. **Worldwide Coordinated effort and Strategy: Tending to Cross-Line Difficulties:**

Numerous natural difficulties rise above public boundaries, requiring worldwide coordinated effort and conciliatory intercessions. Peaceful accords, like the Show on Organic Variety and the Paris Arrangement, epitomize how nations can meet up to address shared natural worries. Looking at worldwide cooperation highlights the significance of aggregate activity in handling issues that require facilitated endeavors on a planetary scale.

14. **Rewilding Drives: Permitting Nature to Recover Its Wild Spaces:**
The idea of rewilding includes permitting nature to recover regions that have been changed by human exercises. Rewilding drives once again introduce cornerstone species, reestablish regular cycles, and make hallways for untamed life movement. Inspecting fruitful rewilding projects gives experiences into how human intercessions can make conditions for biological systems to self-manage and recover their normal equilibrium.

15. **Roundabout Economy: Limiting Waste and Amplifying Maintainability:**
Changing towards a round economy addresses a groundbreaking mediation pointed toward limiting waste and boosting maintainability. Inspecting roundabout economy rehearses uncovers how asset effectiveness, reusing, and the decrease of single-use things can add to the recuperating of biological systems. This all encompassing methodology underscores shutting the circle on material streams, adjusting financial exercises to biological standards.

16. **Agroecology: Blending Agribusiness with Nature's Examples:**
Agroecology epitomizes an agrarian worldview that orchestrates cultivating rehearses with normal environments. Analyzing agroecological mediations shows how regenerative horticulture, agroforestry, and permaculture can advance biodiversity, improve soil wellbeing, and add to environment flexibility. Agroecology shows the potential for human mediations in horticulture to line up with the standards of environmental equilibrium.

17. **Green Framework: Incorporating Nature into Human Spaces:**
Green framework incorporates regular components into metropolitan and modern spaces, giving numerous advantages to the two individuals and the climate. Inspecting green framework drives uncovers how consolidating parks, green rooftops, and metropolitan green spaces can relieve the effects of urbanization, improve biodiversity, and make strong metropolitan environments.

18. **Preservation Brain research: Figuring out Human Way of behaving for Powerful Intercessions:**
Analyzing the field of protection brain research reveals insight into understanding human way of behaving and dynamic with regards to

ecological preservation. Bits of knowledge from this discipline can illuminate intercessions that are customized to address the mental and social elements impacting human associations with environments. By figuring out the inspirations, discernments, and obstructions that profoundly impact conduct, protection brain research upgrades the viability of human mediations in biological system mending.

19. **Corporate Social Obligation: Adjusting Strategic approaches to Natural Stewardship:**

Corporate social obligation (CSR) addresses a type of human intercession where organizations adjust their practices to standards of ecological stewardship. Inspecting CSR drives represents how organizations can add to biological system mending by taking on maintainable inventory chains, decreasing ecological impressions, and supporting protection projects. The joining of CSR into corporate techniques shows the potential for monetary elements to assume a positive part in natural security.

20. **The Job of Resident Science: Drawing in People in general in Information Assortment and Protection:**

Resident science connects with the general population in logical examination and information assortment, encouraging a feeling of local area contribution in protection endeavors. Looking at resident science drives shows the way that outfitting the aggregate force of people can add to huge scope information assortment, checking, and research. Resident science represents the potential for democratizing science and including different networks during the time spent understanding and mending environments.

All in all, looking at the potential for human mediation to mend and safeguard environments uncovers a multi-layered scene of methodologies, developments, and practices that can shape a more reasonable and agreeable concurrence among people and the regular world. From protection rehearses and supportable asset the board to mechanical developments, local area strengthening, and worldwide coordinated efforts, human mediations offer a range of chances to address the difficulties presented by natural debasement.

As we explore the intricacies of this relationship, the basic lies in perceiving the interconnectedness of environments, esteeming biodiversity, and embracing an aggregate liability to be stewards of the planet. Through deliberate and informed mediations, humankind has the ability to be a mending force, guaranteeing the flexibility and imperativeness of environments for current and people in the future.

9.3 Inspiring hope through concrete examples of recovery.

Motivating expectation through substantial instances of recuperation fills in as a strong story that highlights the flexibility of the normal world and the positive effect of devoted preservation endeavors. As the worldwide local area wrestles with ecological difficulties, these accounts of recuperation give motivation as well as important examples on the viability of human mediation in reestablishing environments, restoring species, and encouraging an agreeable conjunction among mankind and the regular world.

1. **The Momentous Bounce back of the Bald Eagle:**
   One famous illustration of recuperation that moves trust is the momentous bounce back of the bald eagle (Haliaeetus leucocephalus) in the US. When confronting the danger of annihilation because of the far reaching utilization of the pesticide DDT, which prompted diminishing eggshells and conceptive disappointment, deliberate preservation endeavors were started.

   The restricting of DDT and the foundation of natural surroundings assurances prepared for the recuperation of bald eagle populaces. In 2007, the bald eagle was eliminated from the jeopardized species list, denoting a critical protection achievement. This story epitomizes how designated mediations, including strategy changes and environment security, can prompt the resurgence of a once-jeopardized animal groups.

2. **The Phoenix of the Seas: Coral Reefs Strength in Palau:**
   Despite worldwide coral reef decline, the narrative of coral reefs in Palau gives an encouraging
   sign. Palau, an island country in the western Pacific, confronted difficulties from environmental change, overfishing, and contamination, prompting the debasement of its coral reefs. In any case, through proactive preservation measures, including the foundation of marine safeguarded regions and severe fishing guidelines, Palau's coral reefs have given indications of versatility. Coral cover has expanded in certain areas, and marine biodiversity has bounced back. This model grandstands the potential for viable preservation approaches to restore and safeguard delicate marine environments, offering expect the recuperation of coral reefs around the world.

3. **The Phoenix of the Seas: Coral Reefs Strength in Palau:**
   Notwithstanding worldwide coral reef decline, the narrative of coral reefs in Palau gives an encouraging sign. Palau, an island country in the western Pacific, confronted difficulties from environmental change, overfishing, and contamination, prompting the corruption of its coral reefs. Be that as it may, through proactive preservation measures, including the foundation of marine safeguarded regions and severe fishing guidelines, Palau's coral reefs have given indications of strength. Coral cover has expanded in certain areas, and marine biodiversity has bounced back. This model features the potential for successful preservation strategies to

resuscitate and safeguard delicate marine environments, offering expect the recuperation of coral reefs around the world.

4. **The Imperiled Iberian Lynx's Striking Rebound:**
The Iberian lynx (Lynx pardinus), one of the world's most imperiled cats, confronted a shaky circumstance with lessening populaces and a contracting environment in Spain and Portugal. Nonetheless, through an engaged protection exertion that elaborate hostage reproducing programs, territory reclamation, and prey the executives, the Iberian lynx has seen a critical expansion in its populace. This example of overcoming adversity features the significance of versatile preservation systems custom-made to the particular necessities of imperiled species. The Iberian lynx's exceptional rebound fills in as an uplifting illustration of how designated mediations can switch the direction of a fundamentally imperiled animal categories.

5. **Resuscitating Stream Biological systems: The Fruitful Reclamation of the Elwha Waterway:**
In the Pacific Northwest of the US, the reclamation of the Elwha Waterway remains as a demonstration of the groundbreaking force of environment rebuilding. The expulsion of two dams on the Elwha Waterway, the Elwha and Glines Ravine Dams, started one of the main dam evacuation and stream reclamation projects ever. The destroying of these dams permitted salmon to recover admittance to their noteworthy producing grounds, prompting a resurgence in salmon populaces. The recuperation stretched out past fish, as other untamed life and plant species returned, and the general strength of the stream environment gotten to the next level. The Elwha Stream reclamation represents how strong intercessions can restore whole biological systems and inhale life back into debased scenes.

6. **The Protection Renaissance of the California Condor:**
The California condor (Gymnogyps californianus) addresses a convincing preservation example of overcoming adversity described by tirelessness and cooperative endeavors. By the late twentieth 100 years, just a modest bunch of California condors stayed in the wild because of lead harming and natural surroundings obliteration. Nonetheless, an aggressive preservation program including hostage reproducing, living space assurance, and public mindfulness crusades was started. Through many years of committed work, the California condor populace has bounced back, and fruitful renewed introductions into the wild have occurred. This renaissance of the California condor delineates how a comprehensive and multidisciplinary approach can safeguard an animal types from the verge of termination.

7. **The Preservation Win of the Middle Eastern Oryx:**
The Bedouin oryx (Oryx leucoryx), a sublime desert gazelle, confronted

up and coming eradication in the wild due to overhunting and territory corruption in Oman. An exhaustive protection program was sent off, consolidating hostage reproducing, environment reclamation, and severe enemy of poaching measures. This coordinated methodology prompted a critical bounce back in the Bedouin oryx populace, and the species was effectively once again introduced into its local natural surroundings. The preservation win of the Middle Eastern oryx exhibits how vital and facilitated endeavors can bring an animal types back from the edge of eradication, offering an outline for protection drives in dry conditions.

8. **The Continuous Recuperation of the European Buffalo: An Image of Rewilding Achievement:**

   The European buffalo (Buffalo bonasus), Europe's heaviest land well evolved creature, confronted annihilation in the wild by the mid twentieth 100 years. Be that as it may, through rewilding drives and coordinated preservation endeavors, European buffalo populaces have been effectively restored in a few nations. The Buffalo Rewilding System includes renewed introductions, natural surroundings reclamation, and local area commitment, adding to the rebuilding of huge herbivore elements in European environments. The continuous recuperation of the European buffalo fills in as an image of rewilding achievement and delineates how human mediations can switch the fortunes of an animal groups and its job in forming environments.

9. **The Kakapo Parrot's Excursion from the Verge of Eradication:**

   The Kakapo parrot (Strigops habroptilus), local to New Zealand, confronted the verge of eradication with just a small bunch of people remaining. A devoted preservation program, including escalated hunter control, territory rebuilding, and a one of a kind reproducing technique, has prompted a sluggish however consistent expansion in Kakapo numbers. The parrot's story embodies the difficulties and triumphs of monitoring fundamentally jeopardized species on islands, where obtrusive hunters represent a critical danger. The Kakapo's excursion from the verge of eradication features the significance of versatile administration and long haul responsibility in species recuperation.

10. **The Fruitful Recuperation of the Dark Wolf in Yellowstone: A Trophic Outpouring Released:**

    The renewed introduction of dark wolves (Canis lupus) to Yellowstone Public Park during the 1990s has turned into a typical case of fruitful species recuperation and the significant effect of cornerstone species. The shortfall of wolves had prompted an overpopulation of elk, bringing about overgrazing and flowing consequences for different species. The renewed introduction of wolves set off a trophic fountain, with benefits flowing through the environment. Vegetation bounced back, helping beavers, birds, and in any event, modifying the direction of streams. The fruitful recuperation of the dim wolf in Yellowstone delineates how the reclamation of a solitary animal types can have flowing constructive outcomes on whole biological systems.

11. **The Restoration of the Tasmanian Villain: Doing combating a Contagious Malignant growth:**
The Tasmanian fiend (Sarcophilus harrisii) confronted a serious danger from a contagious malignant growth known as Demon Facial Cancer Illness (DFTD), prompting a huge decrease in populaces across
Tasmania. Moderates answered with a multi-layered approach, including hostage rearing projects, infection the executives techniques, and public mindfulness crusades. The effective foundation of illness free populaces and the ID of safe people have offered trust for the drawn out endurance of this remarkable marsupial. The narrative of the Tasmanian fiend exhibits the flexibility of species despite arising dangers and the significance of versatile protection measures.

12. **The Recuperation of the Humpback Whale: A Worldwide Preservation Achievement:**

The humpback whale (Megaptera novaeangliae), once chased extremely close to eradication for its fat and oil, has encountered a surprising recuperation following worldwide preservation endeavors. The ban on business whaling, laid out by the Worldwide Whaling Commission in 1986, assumed a significant part in safeguarding humpback whale populaces.

Ensuing preservation measures, for example, the assignment of marine safeguarded regions and guidelines to forestall transport strikes, further added to the species' resurgence. The humpback whale's excursion from risk to assurance exhibits the force of worldwide collaboration in rationing marine megafauna.All in all, the rousing instances of recuperation introduced here exhibit the potential for human mediation to be a power for positive change in the domain of preservation.

These accounts offer a brief look into the strength of species, the viability of preservation procedures, and the expectation that, with purposeful endeavors, environments can be recuperated, and biodiversity can thrive. As we think about these stories, obviously the excursion of recuperation is continuous and requires supported responsibility, development, and coordinated effort. Through gaining from these triumphs, we can move an aggregate feeling of obligation and cultivate a common vision for a future where the recuperation of biological systems and species keeps on being a demonstration of the groundbreaking effect of human commitment to ecological stewardship.